Ex Nihilo

A Book of Poems

ERIC WAYNE FLYNN

ARCHWAY
PUBLISHING

Archway Publishing books may be ordered through booksellers or by contacting:

Archway Publishing
1663 Liberty Drive
Bloomington, IN 47403
www.archwaypublishing.com
1 (888) 242-5904

Because of the dynamic nature of the Internet, any web addresses or links contained in
this book may have changed since publication and may no longer be valid. The views
expressed in this work are solely those of the author and do not necessarily reflect the
views of the publisher, and the publisher hereby disclaims any responsibility for them.

Any people depicted in stock imagery provided by Getty Images are models,
and such images are being used for illustrative purposes only.
Certain stock imagery © Getty Images.

ISBN: 978-1-4808-8721-3 (sc)
ISBN: 978-1-4808-8722-0 (e)

Library of Congress Control Number: 2020901315

Print information available on the last page.

Archway Publishing rev. date: 01/30/2020

Follow the Author:
@ericwayneflynn.com
or
Via 📷 🐦 or 🅕
@ericwayneflynn

CONTENTS

ALIVE

To create or not to create.
To even exist, such an egomaniacal thought.
To play God—for the gift is upon us.
To make something out of nothing.
To take the time to sculpt the materials into a palace.
To falter in trial.
To repeat the process and eventually succeed.
To breathe it all in.
To taste the fruit.
To give birth.
To be born.
To love.
To die.
To be
alive.

IMAGINATION

My childhood friend.
My lifetime lover.
The best company I've ever known.
A thousand failures we've created together.
Without you, I wouldn't be me,
the person I've always tried to escape.
I'm finally settling into this skin.
Tonight, we will stay up late.
Just you and me.

THE DIVER OF THE DEEP

Orange cream sits atop the blue of the bay.
A young father must feed his seed.
And so he must work.
And so he dives down,
down into the deep.
Into the dark.
Into where the monster lives.
Where life is measured in breaths.
The pressure mounts as he dives farther.
Down into the dark with only a drum that beats
black, boom, boom, black.
I hear he couldn't see a thing
except a few specks.
Little flickers of light.
Something to swim for.
But the diver must now fix a net
so his family can eat fish.
Into the net with a knife he goes.
He cuts, he breathes, he rests, he repairs, he thinks,
Swimming to the top is the only way out.
Emerging back in the glow of the orange cream,
victory fills the lungs.
Climbing back on to the boat, the diver collects his pay.
Today his family eats.
Happiness in life managed by the day,
by the weather,
by the window,
watching the rain,
watching his wife.
The diver dives into her.
It's a soft summer night.
There is love in the room;
there is magic in the air.
In just a few moments, a seed will sprout a life that wasn't there.
It's a boy, born afraid to dive.
A coward with a pen
searching for air.

And so he must work.
And so he dives down,
down into the deep.
Into the dark.
Into where the monster lives.
Where life is measured in breaths.

Breaking Windows and Plucking Wildflowers

An aged, old stone
Lay there upon the earth.
An adolescent soul
Possessed by rebirth.
The energy to feel alive
Escaping us from the start.
Billions of beings.
Beams of light.
The stone awaits,
Ready to be thrown.
Showing off for no one, the soul alone.
Tossing the stone up and down in his hand.
What does power feel like?
What is it to be man?
Smash! Boom! Bam!
Right through that window.
The one that reveals an empty garage filled with junk.
Satisfied and coming down from the adventure,
The young soul takes a stroll down to the meadow.
There is a bouquet of fresh-plucked wildflowers.
Destruction can be beautiful.
Whispers from the wind breeze through the air.
Clear and soft, soft enough to hear
A secret.

THE HILL

Watching children ascend upon the hill.

A lonely one, left behind, observes as the others climb.

Many are reaching the top and soon looking around for another sweet soul,

Someone to tell them they are good and to further their sense of achievement.

Assuring they are wonderfully capable of accomplishing all feats as they embark upon this life.

The sun is shining bright upon their faces, and they are comfortable in its light,

Feeling the warmth of their success.

Golden milk from a mother's breast

And a pat on the head from a proud papa.

Looking up at the hill, lost in their shadows, the last, the forgotten, is ready to start its climb.

At the bottom, it desires to feel the same as they.

Young hubris dancing at a party in which it seems it were not invited.

An ache it is, wanting to be on top with the rest,

The beautiful and glamorous ones who get to smile and wave to Mommy and Daddy.

"Look at me! Look at what I can do!"

So the lonely one decidedly takes its first step.

Digging its foot into the face of the hill,

Muscles and mind working on the goal: the climb.

And so it does.

Soon the lonely one is halfway up the hill and overlooking a cliff,

Scarcely holding onto a clump of grass; the thin roots somehow allow it to hold on.

At the bottom, it now sees water crashing into rocks.

It questions why they weren't there before.

Looking back up, it wonders if the others saw the same,

And if this whole challenge is all just a part of some silly game.

Ahh, keep on going! Upward and onward! Don't look down!

Failure isn't an option for the lonely one

For 'tis faith that conquers fear and steers us from the ground.

And so it won't stop climbing.

Up, up, up.

Brown, brown, brown dirt is falling down upon its eye.

A peek of blue then smacks the face, suddenly revealing the sky.

For the lonely one has reached the top.

And with a swivel of the head, it looks around to find some adoration from the others.

But there is none.

So instead of wallowing, the lonely one's head kicks back to focus upon the glory.
The spirits then send praise that no one else can see.
Mere mortals search for skin.
The child's head then lowers in shame,
Questioning while the others dance on by, laughing and enjoying their fruits.
Why had it been set apart?

THE HOUSE WITH A HOOP

Southern skin, headed up north—an abrupt shake.
Five strong against a full-court press, making a fast break.
Laughing and crying in a wood-paneled wagon.
'80s fresh: big hair 'n' Buster Browns; now that's what I call fashion.
The trail blazed; mission accomplished.
'N' there it stood, ten feet tall, and wow, I was astonished.
Wondering, *Now what could that be?*
Instant—its power over me.
"Hmm. It needs something else … a melon? A ball!"
Damn, I couldn't wait to play; ya gotta dribble before ya crawl.
One on none, morning till night, day after day.
One on none; that is, until someone else came to play.
Fun with others, learning about competition.
I was addicted, in love, developing a condition.
Put to the test, *Let's see where I stand?*
The competition growing greater, punishing and ridiculing, so I question, "I, a man?"
Fuel.
Spark.
Fuel.
Fire.
Fuel.
Raging.
Fuel.
Desire.
Challenged and bullied, now did I learn to show my teeth?
Nah, keep 'em concealed; withhold thy weapon, so my mouth becometh my sheath.
So after years of tears and years of fears, it seemed my beloved had no love for me.
"What's the score? Oh, Team Upset is down by two? Then I'll step back for three."
And so I made it.
Not on the court; I'm talking out here in the streets,
Learning what it is to lose and understanding how to deal with defeat.
And through all this, the fundamentals of the relationship have never changed.
Swish or *Cachunk,* nylons or chains.
Love so pure and beautiful it's lyrical.
The rim, a halo, it's spiritual.
A lifelong romance; you've taught me so much.
You made me better; you developed my touch.

And still, I go on dates with you, just the two of us, blessed.
Take away some pain and some fear, while alleviating some stress.
And so till my dying day, you may find me laying it up somewhere … kick the bucket?
Nope. Attacking it and finishing with a scoop.
Wood-paneled wagon full of poor southern skin headed for the house with a hoop.

Hollow

Stumbling through a thick brush near the ocean,
A version of myself searches for a place to call my own.
Cool green leaves slap my face.
I push on.
A clearing awaits, and I see the rays of the sun pouring down into a big brown hole.
I jump in and am quickly surrounded by four walls of dirt.
I mash some cold earth in my hand.
There's a chair in my hole, a rock, and an old red door.
I pick up the malleable wood and lean it against the wall facing the ocean.
It would be nice to enter here with the blue at my back.
I then place my chair in a corner facing the red door.
It's a sturdy chair; it does its job.
Next, I roll my rock out of the hole and into the sun.
Hopping on top my rock, I feel the temperateness on my skin.
I'm alone now and finally have a place to call my own.
Back down into my hole I go.
I walk around a bit, thinking,
I cleaned up this big ol' ditch real darn good.
I'm proud of it.
I can't wait to have my friends over.
I'm going to serve candy, chips, and orange soda.
Welp … my mom 'n' pop will be looking for me soon; I better get going.
Plus I miss my brother and sister.
We're having chicken, mashed potatoes, and green beans tonight.
Better crawl out of this hole and head on home.
Now I know that at the very least I have somewhere to go if it all falls apart.

CARAMEL POPCORN POWER-UP

When I was eight or so, my brother and I went across the street to my neighbor's.
Our buddy Jen had a Nintendo and a bunch of different games.
We were all playing Mega Man, or Mike Tyson's Punchout, or something or other,
And another boy was there. Not sure who he was; can't remember a name or face.
But I do remember a large tub of caramel popcorn.
A, B, A, B, A, B equated to a lot of jumping or punching; I can't recall which.
But I do remember a large tub of caramel popcorn.
We all dove into the sweet crunch.
Then … more jumping and punching, punching or jumping; again, I don't recall.
Time-out for another handful.
As we all continued playing and munching, jumping and/or punching,
The nameless, faceless boy kept devouring more and more popcorn—more than his
fair share.
No one objected, but energy soon dictated that he explain himself to the group.
He claimed, "I need it. It gives me a power-up to play better."
The rationale didn't make any sense; well, not to us at least.
But once again, no one objected, so he continued to dive into the tub.
And the crunch he made with his mouth annoyed the shit out of me, damn swine.
If we were in a prison camp, he'd a eaten more beans, apples, bread, or whatever the
rations were, would, or *will* be.
Not a great general either; we'd have performed a mutiny.
Anyway, we were children, and it wasn't war or prison or famine.
It was a hot summer day in 1987, and we had a big tub of caramel popcorn.
Why do I recall such a petty insignificance?
Well, he *was* playing the game at a better clip.
'N' I thought maybe he does need it more than me, my brother, or Jen.
That was the day I was introduced to the placebo effect.
Either that or a natural-born bullshitter.

BEER CAN MATTRESS
FLASHBACK

A door to the past is ajar in my mind.
I then twist and shove it open to see
A war criminal, a prisoner of the war,
Wanting another beer upon his bed and nothing more.
So he screams aloud to yonder door
Where I now stand,
Looking at the mirror, seeing the mirror, but something's missing.
The man,
Lying slack now, festering in the sun,
Palms up to the trees, pleading
On his back for us, bleeding.
Young minds certainly do die young
Out in the jungle, dwelling upon what it is they had done—and why.
As questions come fast and harsh,
Do I? Do we? Why do we die? Die, do we?
Soul of the 60s, trapped in the jungle,
Lying in a room upon a beer can–covered mattress
Demanding,
"Kid, get me a beer!"
Me, being the man I am now, asking my younger self,
"Why didn't you adhere?"
He'd probably say, "Because of the fear."
I had enlisted
A night in my friend's haunted house.
We slept, fatigued from the day at play
As the man from the war then went to it,
Threatening murder, arson, and pain
To all who had slept in the jungle and not paid their dues.
The price: The one he saw fit.
I knew the man was crazy,
And if I ever get to see another hero,
I'll recognize the broken product
Out of the package and handled.
A toy,

A man,
A victim,
A killer
Adrift upon a beer can–covered mattress.
I dart home.
I retreat.
Forget the smell of victory.
I like the taste of defeat
For I will live to fight another day.
I soon arrive back at my childhood home.
"Who left a goddamn spoon in the sink?"
Back in the trenches I go.
My trivial world.
Thank you,
To all the men who served on a beer can–covered mattress.

UNDER THE IRON FIST

Walking on eggshells
Under suburban rule,
Tipsy,
Tiptoeing in the night,
Drunk on the moon.
A battle for the ages between blood must now resume.
The old hound, sensing something afoot, rises from slumber
As the young pup, sneakily dodging creaky boards memorized in recon, strikes a frozen pose.
Undetected, he then hears the stream of the ruler against the throne.
Flushed cheeks in the kitchen, bare-assed in the bath, the ruler finishes his business.
The din of a squeaky hinge in suburbia then reveals the ruler with his staff in hand.
Scratching his head, he spots the youth.
Parentally paralyzed, frozen in blue moonlight, the youth surrenders,
Accepting the weight that will come with the morning.
Son versus father, father versus son—a fight, a call to arms.
A lifetime war of preparation for the coldest winters and the hardest truths.
As the devil lay within all men and within their very blood,
No man will bring the other more fear than that which each possesses for the other.
Distorted mirror images in a haunted house—reflecting ghosts of the past, present, and future—
Scared till death that they just might be one in the same.
Eye to eye they meet, dog ready to eat dog.
Love, respect, and admiration boiling in their chests.
Understanding, left for a cold day on the battlefield,
When the white flags have all been waved and all the battles fought,
A toast to all those nurtured in such a way as this.
A toast to all those raised under the iron fist.

ASPHYXIATION

Choking.
A white picket fence is lodged in my throat.
Wooden stakes driven into my head and my heart,
Splintering into my flesh,
Are slowly forming festering sores that keep my mind from rest.
And soon this false ideal is a metal pail that hangs nailed unto my chest—
Filled with shit, piss, and blood—
Hanging from white bone and a wooden white beam,
accompanied by other thick fluids lost from twelve rounds of the American dream.
The one that used to keep me up all night,
Slapping me around and cutting off my oxygen.
Yes.
These ropes or the hands of the ghosts that choke,
That stifle and scare us stiff.
Well now… while I'm unraveling,
I can see you across the street, a perfect square,
Fitted for a long rectangle, standing there with your thumb up your ass,
Wondering what to do as the air slips away.

IF I NEVER LEFT TOWN

From the womb to the room,
The playground, the neighborhood,
To the outskirts, to the edge,
The end of an era.
Home, just another thing to turn your back on.
Into the wild, into the unknown,
Into a 1965 Ford filled to the brim, foot upon the gas,
Accelerating into the future, back to the past.
Hands on the wheel, windows down, radio up.
In a rush, in a fog, figuring a way out,
Arriving at a certain time, a certain place.
The boy behind the wheel, driven to search for the man,
Looks in his rearview and extends to the child a hand,
Waving it in the air, saying his last goodbyes,
Surfing upon the wind as the tears roll down his eyes
For a dream is fading in the mirror.
The man, now solo behind the wheel,
Has left the child in the dust—this dark forest—
To dig itself a ditch so it has a place to sleep.
Now!
Both of you!
Fend!
Show you can make a go of it alone!
Fight!
Learn to survive this impasse all upon your own.
Man upon the road.
Boy within the woods.
Man immersed in evil.
Boy inundated in good.
No gray, no middle-ground.
'Tis the balance of extremes—the yin and the yang,
The tightrope, the seesaw, the pendulum.
The noose
Tied to a tree in the woods, haunting the child's brain.
Meanwhile, the man behind the wheel feels the world's grip, its vice, and all its pain
Subverting their natures, playing games with their heads.
In the light, in the dark, through the fire, voices then said,

"What happens if he to fail?
What happens if he to fall?
What happens if he to lose?
What happens to us all?"
The legend tells us we all have wings, yet, still, we are afraid to fly.
The boy's old Ford filled with junk, empty comforts, weighing him down before he to die.
"Look at me! I made it," 'tis what each of us dreams to say.
Boy and the man, struggling to control the wheel, swerving in the dark, searching for the day
When the sun cuts through the fog, dicing it into a fine spectrum of mist.
Hunting for this, for that, in which we all wish to achieve
Happiness, a temporary rainbow, a hidden answer granting the reprieve.
Off the road, hovering above the grave, over there in the sand.
The line drawn for the boy, introduced by the hands of man,
Erasing,
Eroding,
Decaying.
Into a diner,
A coffee cup is withering in my hand.
I take a sip.
Inside my head, it's swimming all around.
Digging through this collection of debris,
I sit and sip, marveling upon the journey and reveling in all these things that I've found.
Yes, I sit, and I sip, wondering,
Who is it that I would be if I never left town?

WAVES

Energy comes in waves,
Changing the landscape,
Allowing progress through erosion.

PROVIDENCE

A wonderful place for a poser to hide
Until one finds their groove.
Or better yet, hits their stride.
Then, and only then, will it feel like a happy home.
Nurturing,
Inspiring even.
At times celestial but still of the flesh.
A good day spa, rubbing out the kinks, making good of this mess.
Small and strong, it knows its place.
Beautiful and lovely, filled with sweetness, flowers, and grace.
Like a good woman, she will give you what she gets.
But I—just another shadow, lurking, dreaming of New York—
Wishes for greater things while surrounded by this benevolent welfare,
Yearning for *more*.
What a cheat! A louse!
This beautiful matrimony between flesh and concrete upon me, and still I search
for a spouse?
Something better?
Ah, you fool!
Divinity is here within the palms of your hands!
Please, someone slap some sense into me.
Ah, it's a sunflower on Angell Street shining as I walk on by,
Woolgathering about Rome,
Watching the Western world rise.
I'm at the Coliseum, and I've an extra-large nacho.
A man is fighting a lion named Life.
Excessive when granted Providence every day.

Sometimes It's Just Snow

Sometimes it's just snow.
Even words from Frost can fall short and numb.
Flakes of beauty that evaporate on hot hoods.
The wear of winter on every face
Bundled up for the fight.
Decidedly, I pierce my ears with some sounds.
Evans is tickling me with his touch,
Changing my tune.
I enjoy the fragile flakes' fall from heaven.
There is a metaphor here somewhere, but who cares?
I'm going to settle down and watch the white majesty
As children build men in our honor.
I will soon be added to the scenery.
But for now, I shall sip a hot drink.
Sometimes it's just snow.
I keep telling myself this, but I know better.

Human

The only race that matters.
Differences, but destined for the same finish line.
All of us crouched, ready to run, awaiting the sound of the gun.
Have enough sense to enjoy the colorful landscape.
The petty, without character, will dart by in haste.
Don't sweat the small stuff.
We will see them at the end,
Jockeying for position, recognition, and applause,
Heralding themselves triumphant over the other.
Adorned with flowers that they never could smell,
Unwilling to testify unto their own explicit form of inferiority
As we celebrate each other for ours,
Awaiting our most cherished reward.

HAPPINESS

A victim of confused catalysis,
Never the wiser,
Never an achieved destination.
A rest stop filled with smiles.
A warm wind that visits but never resides.

INNOCENCE

When it's lost, it's lost,
Never again to return.
Douse this fire that is purity,
And feel what it is to burn.
Be cool, chill.
Don't worry, ye precious little soul, it ain't nothing but a stain.
Say farewell to the angel that you were, and learn to live within the pain.
The knowing
This experience
An early taste of death.
The elixir,
This drug,
Heavy upon thy baby's breath.
An open mouth kissed,
Lips parted,
A hand between the legs.
Flesh exposed in fantasy
Slowly forms the addict,
And now, baby, you start to beg.
And then you begin to fade and forget
All the spectacular things you once did,
All the beauty and love that you made,
The raw flower that you were
When you were just a kid.

SHE

That is woman.
A body,
A force,
A rebel.
A weapon
Between her legs.
Behind her eyes,
A mystery
Open to interpretation.
She,
Malevolent and kind,
Tender and cruel,
A beloved necessity.
And still …

I Would Like to Think

I would like to think there is a place in your heart,
A warm, soft, spot that has never been touched residing behind a wall of ice.
I would like to think I could melt it with a fiery brush of my lips.
Too bold? Too soon?
Instead of a kiss, I'll arrange words to make you swoon,
So rather than melt the wall, you'll throw over a ladder.
A doweled permit to climb to the top and consider your secret garden.
Watching from this safe distance, I spy a sight for sore eyes.
To never fall again, I swore,
'N' I would like to think you swore the same lie,
Protesting to the stars and pounding on your pillow,
Whispering to Cupid to save his arrows for another fool.
I would like to think I could make you believe again.
Not in love, not in lust, but in life.
The purest of emotions and long walks chaperoned by great conversation.
Sunny days by the ocean, a picnic, and catching fireflies after dark.
Beautiful little notions sprinkled with innocence; rekindled naivete lost from a
broken heart.
I would like to think if we were ever to meet again, face-to-face,
We would create a spark to be shared in our stare,
And my hands would then run through your hair, down to your rosy-red cheeks.
Oh, how our wild hearts would beat, beat, beat.
We, kindred spirits with truly no need to speak.
I would like to think.
I think too much.
Sweet thoughts oft fool me, sweet thoughts oft not be true.
But I would like to think you would catch me if I fell in love with you.

A Slow Burn

Balance change.
Remain true
For not a pretentious whim.
A wave that fails to reach the shore,
Trapped in and upon the ocean and all its depths.
The immense weight of liquid life
Flooding my being.
Pretty brown eyes.
Beauty can float.
A creature in the dark.
In this cold, keep warm by me.
Assume we want the devil.
Proclaim we are the truth,
Valor inside that of the rose.
Tulips and kisses for the giver of life.
Love, challenged upon all rocks.
Strength to live,
To lift,
To light
The flame.
A candle,
A conversation,
Knowledge of each other.
Truth and salvation.
A slow burn.

SILENT HARMONY

Running through the streets,
Running through me,
A strength, coagulated.
The mere thought of you
Burning beside,
Twisting and turning.
Flames inside and out.
We blend,
We burn,
We melt.
We are sweet cream,
And it's together that we rise.
Blessed, the best we can be.
Me inside of you,
You inside of me.
But see this: We never even touch.
It's a silent harmony,
A passive truth,
The blind man's stare.
A submissive vision sealed with a kiss.
An orange-colored sky, peaches 'n' cream, a midsummers night's bliss,
If only to be found somewhere in each other's grace.
Somewhere in the ether, not of a tangible place.
Then you'd see that we can soar, and gravity be damned.
You, an ordinary woman,
I, an ordinary man.
And it's extraordinary, this glory to be shared.
And yet our names are a whisper through the trees.
A murmur to our souls as we fall upon our knees.
And its here the healing can now begin.
Rebirth unto the body through this recollection of sin,
And somewhere running through the streets is dark honey.
Blood dashing through its recognized course.
The fated echoes of the past at an increased frequency, a staggering rate.
The beat,
The pulse,
The heart,

The soul.

A love

Unconditional; that shall be the only condition in this test.

Thus we learn from experience and our aspirations, these drawings of ambitious breaths.

The stars aligned, waiting to shine

In that one certain moment,

A written destiny scribbled inside the finite possibility of shared space.

Two Shooting Stars

Let's take a ride.
Recline your seat, and put your feet up on the dash.
Venus to Mars, we can soar in a flash.
Listen,
No roads to steal your voice.
Altitudes high, higher than high.
Off we go, far past the ethereal mist.
No one can see us from below,
And yet, we do exist.
Thrown into the atmosphere,
Spiraling out of control.
Worried, confused, giddy with fear.
Unseen by the human eye, unheard by the human ear,
And yet, we do exist.
Two shooting stars.
No one knows how bright we are.
Wish you weren't afraid to fall and shine with me.
Then everyone could see
Two shooting stars.
Yet, we do exist.
When will we realize this?
We are
Two shooting stars.

THE LUCKY ONES

All at once, truly, in the blink of an eye,
Out of thin air an appearance, an angel from the sky.
Instant to feel blessed, well within grace,
A soldier of love fallen victim unto the sight of a face.
Crawling in from the battlefield, a bleeding heart, man, always in need of repair.
Casualty after casualty, unrequited, testify in the name of love, so we challenge, so we dare
To ask, to plead, to beg to be loved—the one thing that can save the soul.
Down by the river, speeding recklessly, two bodies out of control.
A dangerous agreement it is, bathing each other in sin.
All the world a blur, chemicals rushing while fate is sinking in.
Yes, destiny it be, down deep, the teeth, lust altered into love on a romantic summer night.
Two falling passionately, hopelessly, this pulsing performance be their rite.
A declaration, a vow, echoing in eternity; the offspring comes of the blood.
What we make of this world, we make together through destruction.
What we make of it is love.

MERCY

Young flowers
Blooming at their own rhythms,
Opening to God.
Life pried open and abused.
Where there is breath, there is violence.
And then there is sex and death
As love lay weeping, unfulfilled, detached,
Suffering under the weight of another's will.
A driving force
Born of wrath,
Fueled by fate,
Claims another victim.

BLUE

You, wrapped up in me; me, wrapped up in you.
We together, together entwined, we, wrapped up in blue.
An old blanket we shared that kept us warm
In our time of need,
In our deep sea, our emotional abyss,
Diving into each other,
Sharing our wave.
My little boy holding hands with your little girl.
On a summer night, speeding down the road again to our river of pain.
Teardrops pelting the windshield, salty and wet, blending with the rain.
Two fools down at the river's edge.
Our little boy and our little girl decide to take a dip
Holding the little girl in his hands,
The little boy morphs into a man,
Making sure she does not drown,
Knowing that she must learn to swim.
Letting go of his mermaid, he knows he shall never see her again
For the experience would be too cruel.
The two, now on separate planets—
Venus and Mars—apart but still of each other's universe.
Yet slowly becoming figments, fragments, pieces of red blown into black.
Cold flows, love goes down into the deepest part of you.
Somewhere lost in the night, the little boy and little girl lie naked,
Nestled in their blanket of blue.

THE BURDEN

Knowing you.
Laying heavy,
The animal—
Ignorant by grace,
Devoid of sin,
Instinct,
Pardoned,
Permission
Granted—
And so I give in.
Never a word of this.

FALLING

Purity
Unto perversion,
Cradle to the grave.
Truth
Unto deception,
The bed that we made—
To love another.
The equation of choice.
Minus the minutiae
Plus the gist,
Division be the voice.
The killing
Good.
Delicious even.

INTEGRITY OF THE HEART

We used to make love.
Now we only make excuses.
In an attempt to be cool, aloof,
We leave out the heat, the flame,
Passion,
Mercy,
Understanding.
This essence that is life
Be none other than thyself
Out in nature,
Naturally, with you
In the midst of the clouds.
On the edge,
At the ledge,
Laughing at an idea.
An ideal—letting go of all that holds us back.
A sacrifice.
So you think you still remember how to fly?

WOMEN OF THIS WORLD

A boy is lying in bed as fantasy begins to fill his mind.
Long stems are wrapping around it.
A flower in bloom is entering his room.
Sweet nectar begins to drip from petal to lips.
Mesmerized by her hips, trying to get a grip
On the women of this world.
Puzzles in pieces, curved and colorful shapes,
Ready to be manipulated, guided, and coerced.
Wanting us men to figure them out, begging us to get a clue.
I think I at least have an idea.
Trying it out, taking the hint.
The flower opens, allowing love to enter.
Love—being a dick, per usual,
Torturing, tantalizing, tempting
The women of this world,
Seducing our senses with nonsense.
Captive and helpless against her flower power.
She asks so little in reality,
Sitting on the windowsill, longing for the admiration of the sun,
Wishing to be understood
Or watered so to stimulate growth.
Always wanting something of light.
I lie in bed and watch the women of this world
Decay and wilt away from me,
Realizing the bed where they had bloomed
A cold climate unsuitable to sustain a life.

BOOKS

Painful pages.
Flowers pressed between them.
Flipping through fine vellum for tender moments,
I grow accustom to their prose.
And pressed between my parchment lay a rose.
Thorns as big as shark's teeth
Shredding up the flesh.
Thumbing through the carnage—next chapter.
The setting: the moon.
Somehow, I am drenched in sweat.
I am naked and alone and bleeding.
Perusing through all these books,
Staining the pages that I love.
Invaluable lessons that will soon mean so very little to me.
Reading too much into them,
Knowing you will eventually relinquish them back to the shelf.

THE BEAT

Wallowing, restlessly rolling around in blankets of self-pity.
Red machines, pumping, running on E in the heart of the city.
Dimly lit rooms of angst harbor fallen soldiers,
Licking their wounds from the battlefields of love.
Veterans of the war, once rookies till Cupid came by and gave them a shove.
Immersed, swimming in deep thoughts of heated actions from their past.
For every million victories in love, there's a billion more that never survive the crash.
Never the lesser, love lingers on, chemicals capturing the brain, holding it hostage,
Seducing and enabling the pain, a chained heart with no locksmith.
Adding colors, textures, and smells to the mirage for truly it never exists.
A manifestation of self, broadcast onto others,
Channeling our reception of how we want to be seen.
We view ourselves only through the eyes of the beholder.
While the greatest war rages on inside, every day a battle with a mirror or a scale.
Under the knife of vanity, we all bleed, scarred debutantes, chasing perfection.
Falling short, skinning our knees, soliciting unto exteriors due to interiors we feel inferior,
We peddle our bodies and do as we are sold.
Our minds and souls never gracing our covers,
Too scared to show what lay inside.
Self-loathing imbeciles afraid of our own shiny shadows.
Learn to love one's self, to display your inner truth.
The only validation you need is a ticket in your possession.
Punch it!
For the ones who truly love themselves are never alone.
And a heart simply cannot love another heart till it loves the beat of its own.

RAINDROPS

The rain is so dramatic.
If you listen close enough,
One can hear
Cackling from afar.
This laugh,
Those cries,
That tear
Burning inside your eye,
Nothing but a raindrop.
Nothing but a raindrop.
Nothing but a raindrop.
A raindrop.
Now you're all wet.
You say, "See to it you don't forget
It ain't nothing but a raindrop."

CALCULATED MADNESS

Plotting and scheming,
A doting beauty is lying upon her back and dreaming.
So in that she can be free
To tell herself the lie; she is in love with thee,
The world and everything in it.
Trapped in her skin, her cards.
Girl had a full house up in that brain.
Girl had a dungeon in her attic.
Cobwebs and mirrors, barrel jugs filled with pain.
And porcelain skin with high cheekbones,
A rosy-red complexion with freckles and an attitude all her own.
A bright sun with a dark side.
A blue moon, a melancholy tide,
Ebbing and flowing;
A beautiful victim of circumstance caught up in it.
What is one to do?
Call out for help?
A life raft—something to hold on to so one does not drown.
Fingernails in my back, dragging me into the ocean, and now I'm sinking down
Into the abyss; well yes, that's where we had to go,
To the core.
Still silence.
Eventually, we can hear our hearts beating in the darkness.
We then begin tenderizing each other,
Manipulating the flesh,
Making a mockery of love.
There is malice on our lips,
Hunger in our eyes,
Lies on our tongues,
Meat inside our teeth and claws,
Madness in our minds.

LET GO OF ME

I've been yours for quite some time now.
We've made love in the morning sun, on rainy afternoons, and on snow-filled nights,
Holding hands throughout all these different atmospheres.
We were so very much in love, and yet, no one was truly aware
Of our passion and how I cut myself open just so you could see me bleed.
Oh, how I walked to the end of the earth for you, and yet, you knew I was doing it for me,
Using you to lean on, nowhere else to turn, I was needy; I am a child, I need to be free
If only to be reborn to come back to life to love you again.
If only you could see how much I truly need you, my lover, my friend.
My everything, I give you my all; I press hard to make you feel my love.
I was lucky enough to have you if only for the night, keeping me company, my candle.
But our affair carried on and on.
Our stories shall burn eternally.
Even right now I'm thinking of you.
Only you!
Why do you matter so much to me?
Why do I have to be in your world to breathe?
To feel alive, something you have given back to me.
I can have nothing and still be my happiest when I'm with you.
But still, I need a break.
I'm beating you to the point where you're dead in my arms,
A pile of pulp.
Oh, what have I done?
You kill what you love,
Inflicting pain upon it because somehow, you're numb, and you need to feel something.
So in your absence, instead of hurting you, I'll take myself out of the equation
And step to a ledge; looking over the edge, I see it's about three miles down.
I've heard them say that you die before you even hit the ground.
Cool.
You don't have to feel the thud.
But if you let go of me, I promise I will come back to you with wings,
And it will be just you and me again.
And we will be better.
We will be back, and we will be more genuine than before.
Please, just let go of me, and I won't go anywhere, I swear.
Just let me fall for a while.
Let me be me.

Let me float.
Let me fly.
Let's take a chance and see if I
Find something new to bring back to you.

CHASING SEAGULLS IN THE SAND

Long forgotten are the days of our star-crossed romps.
They all bleed and coagulate, sticking like wet photos.
Moments captured in a flash, released in a blink.
Fleeting fancies, chewed-up bubblegum jammed under a desk.
Yet, one day remains.
Spring had invited us out to lunch on a desolate beach,
And here we feasted upon each other
As a light breeze was a cool, rewarding sheet against our skin.
The sun and the clouds played peekaboo, as did we, always, eternally.
Soon, a young boy and girl found their way unto us from out of the shadows.
They told us of stories we were never to repeat.
No, they were simply for us; they were ours to keep.
With gained trust, seagulls then began to gather close by.
The girl and the boy, with mischief ablaze in their furnaces, stared each other in the eye,
Challenging, Who is quicker? Who more cunning?
Ready, set, go!
Two darts were then screaming for the bullseye, losing balance in the sand and the wind.
The gulls—experts of the escape—squawked and laughed as they took to the sky.
Free for only a moment, but sometimes that's enough to survive.
Our youth then lay on the sand, gasping, smiling, understanding.
Yes, my dear, this is as good as it is going to get for us.
And with a salty kiss, the children were then washed out to sea,
Drowning forever in potential.
No need for bells without the evidence of bodies.
Wreckage lay hidden in the deep to this day,
Buried treasures in the hearts of the young.
The two star-crossed lovers were then left on shore with only their ghosts,
Holding each other tight as they sobbed and said their goodbyes.
Regrets are for souls who haven't ever loved.
I regret to say,
"I'm not sure."

THE BOY LEFT KISSING THE WIND

Out upon thy lawn, an innocent, enchanted scene
For all is lost in love; 'tis love, or so it seems.
From my window, young love I see amiss.
Eyes gazing at each other, and then, a fate-sealing kiss.
A wet dream, they set a sail for two
Out upon thy lawn, two blades, cutting in the dew.
The sweet liquid from their sweethearts reigns.
Swimming in emotion, lust drags us under, the fair pair in pain.
So be it thy cross to save a sacred soul.
The catalyst, long before this kiss, takes its toll.
It's dowry, a price we pay in blood.
For what won't a poor boy do, will a poor boy do for love?
To show the way, teach one how to feel.
For love doth exist; I've seen it before, and it is real.
It is a round, it is a bout, a peculiar place to find
Out upon thy lawn, for this is love, and so, it must be mine.
My tale, tucked away, a story trapped inside the two.
A question doth come with love; the answer we wish we knew.
Why must the petal be plucked time and time again?
A lost soul must pay for its desecrations; thorns inflict the hearts of men.
And yes, I am just a boy, a boy I have forever been.
Out upon thy lawn, 'tis I, always the boy left kissing the wind.

She Not Made for Thee

Now, if anyone objects.
I say I—if I shall be so bold.
For shall we test the heart of man
As he stands trial and testifies to that 'tis love.
Surely, yes, man can love many the flower.
And if so, see that he chose a rose.
But see this; a tulip shall bloom just the same,
And truly a lily could work just as well, I suppose.
Perhaps any petal can dull the pain.
So should I have to forgo this dance alone?
If not, then yes, I beguile a dance with you.
Standing off to the side is I, the other flower, out of focus and out of view.
But yes, a rose is still a rose, I suppose, even if it goes by another name.
These distant stars, I wish, I wander, and in my heart you remain
An angel from on high in my time of need.
Grace be granted.
Testify.
I say, "Tell the truth of love!"
Convince me of this notion, and I disappear into the ether
To silently watch you from afar.
Away, alone, this pining fool; I close my eyes, and there you are.
Your spirit accompanying me in my dream
For here be the earthly dilemma.
Is this love everything you say it seems?
If so, I applaud this truth,
This sacred union; usurp all these demons that I fed.
For I am a culprit, a criminal; let there be a ransom upon my head.
The audacity, the gall, to trample upon the name of love.
This force, this wave of passion to set us free.
For if I be so mistaken, let the wrath of love do what it must; let it have its way with me,
And I shall be exiled, cast away to an island.
And from this prison my attempts to escape shall be foiled by the hands of fate.
Yes, my fanciful ornate words doomed to the depths of the sea.
Floating to the bottom of the ocean,
These letters in red ink:
Blood be my oath, blood be my decree.
She not made for thee, old boy, she not made for thee.

KICKING ROCKS AND SKIPPING STONES

Down by the lake, on a walk all alone,
Down by the lake, kicking rocks, and skipping stones.
I see people at play out in the sun, carefree upon a boat.
Out in the middle of the blue, I see you, and you're playing too.
Everyone has got a beer, and the music is loud,
Pop poison, polluting brain waves.
Seems possibility is all you can see on a clear day.
Time is on your side, and so is life.
It is grand, and who would take that away?
But believe me, it goes,
Jumping out of the boat and down into the deep.
Underneath the party lies a demon fast asleep,
Waiting to devour you; hell, it's already taken a chunk out of me.
But I am a warrior—all these merciless battles that I've been through.
What will happen when reality comes from out of the deep and then smacks the shit out of you,
Leaving you out cold on a boat in the middle of the lake?
Sadly, I can feel a darkness growing inside me, but make no mistake,
I see you all, leftovers, out to lunch, going to brunch, and then buying the new Galaxy.
The one that's got a huge screen with megapixels;
It makes all our ordinary lives look so glamorous.
And I see you, ready to strike a pose, asking where the camera is.
While back on shore, 'tis I, taking a picture of you.
A Polaroid to prove I'm out of touch, and you're still out of view.
But see this: I know that the monster sleeps in the middle of the lake.
Soon enough, it comes; it awaits, ready to gobble up all the pretty little things.
Isn't it beautiful?

A LIFETIME OF APPEASEMENT

The glitz and the glamour,
The bells 'n' whistles,
Take them away.
Now, what are you left with?
Across the table,
In the bed,
Within your arms.
Behold the stranger,
The person you've come to "love"
Stripped down to the bone,
Exposed,
Subjected to nature.
The walls are closing in.
The paintings and pictures tumbling down.
A hole in the earth developing, engulfing your possessions, a golden tomb in the ground.
Buried,
Yet somehow you both remain.
And now all there is left to do is look each other in the eye and revel in the pain,
The knowing of all things false,
All things built upon sand.
Now, go before each of you sink.
You knew the deal.
You've got all the receipts stashed somewhere in a shoebox,
Souvenirs of times gone by.
Little pieces of paper; invoices accounted for by the lie.

WOLVES O'ER THE LAMB

Tricked, fooled,
Learned, schooled.
Burned by the flame, but the flame has cooled.
Savage dogs about, thirsty in the night, were searching for blood
As a feeble lamb, finding its footing, 'twas out looking for love,
Seduced by the lies of a lover gone astray, this yarn spun coldly behind the lamb's back.
The inexperienced fool, lured before the dogs by this Jezebel, unwitting of their attack.
The game of love, played and now lost, for yes, the lamb had surely been bit
As the dogs of the night, gauging the scar from afar, laughed.
"So this is the Romeo? Ha, little lamb, he ain't shit!"
Sprung upon!
Quickly, grappled by the leader of the pack, tossed and thrown mercilessly to the ground.
The omega struggles to get on top of the alpha as the betas howl and gather round.
Somehow, the lupine leader's fur is pressed against the earth under the weight of the lamb.
The pack, lurking, is soon commissioned by the bitch to carry out the finality of her plan.
And so, bite after bite, their teeth and claws dig into their prey's thin young skin.
No tears can come from the lamb as he won't allow the harsh reality of his sacrifice
to sink in.
No! No! Please! Not a minute more of this can the poor lamb withstand.
Purple and pink, pulped meat stinks, inducing the appetite, the rising of the glands.
And now, the light is getting dim, dimmer, as hope seems nowhere in sight.
But wait!
The shepherd has arrived, and so the wolves then scatter, fearing his wrath and his might.
His staff, his judgment, his love shall now be surely carried throughout the land.
Anointed in a pool of blood, barely breathing, salvation granted,
The lamb now a ram.

AMNESIA

I know her.
Yes, her, there, brooding in her tower,
Deep within her thoughts,
Crushing everything with her mind.
Burying me with her body,
Enticing others with her eyes,
I can now only find her in a dream.
Haunted memories,
Twisted, impassioned lies,
These ghosts we used to be.
With thanks to her, 'twas destiny I was to see.
Our darkness, a glimpse unto the other side.
For life was a placebo,
And thus death she so prescribed.
Further, darker, yes, deeper I went
Into her velvety red pit,
Where the beasts were unleashed
And yet tethered to each other about the neck.
And yet, once imprisoned by the flesh through this spirit, I was freed and can now
recollect.
I know her.
I knew her.
I forget.

NUMB

To feel again
Something new.
Face up to acceptance.
Back unto the fold.
A vast sea
Unto the future.
Swimming in space,
Free,
To well up with hope
As we fathom escaping our destiny,
As we make our world.
We must make it
As we make ourselves,
Numb.

Low

This place I had to go.
Just how far, only I can know.
I'm talking low.
How deep can one sink? Well, let me show ya.
Playing the game, wait, hold on, timeout! Nice to know ya.
Time to fade away, off into the sunset, off into the shadows, off into the trees.
Light fading from my eyes, my heart, my soul; time running out on me.
When, in reality, it was catching up.
My shadow wandering in my fugue, my out-of-body experience; I seemed to have
lost my mind.
Underneath it all—rummaging, digging inside myself to find
Thyself for it is thyself that I must know.
Don't look at me; I don't exist, so just let me go.
Low,
Beneath the surface, the prim exterior, the superficial, down into a melancholy dream,
Floating in a bubble of agony, where no one can hear me scream.
Calling out to the devil, calling out to God, calling out to you.
You all saw me drifting, but what was one to do?
Helpless spectators exposed to a grotesque display.
A mutiny, self-mutilation, destruction be the order of the day.
The beautiful boy prince, a vagabond molding into a man made of virtue and good.
Falling down, farewell ego, the pedestal from which he once stood.
Falling down unto the murderer who lurks at the bottom of the pit.
The murderer in me, the mirror, my image, I must succumb to it.
Under the knife, held in my own hands,
Carving up and out, a new me, a new man,
Disgusted by the suffering written across his face.
So
Low,
Where I had to go for just a taste
Of death, of truth, of reality.
A few things I had to study.
A few things I had to experience.
A few things I had to figure out.
A few things in which I still am yet to know.
Dust settling down upon a nightstand, and here we are together.
Low.

THE BUILDING AND THE BOY

Surrounded by brick,
Back in a dream,
Questioning reality,
I look out my window from the second floor.
Seems to me there is a flood,
Memories taking form in a cool gray liquid.
Brick, my canvas.
Brick, my bone.
A madman lives on the second floor, hollowed out and all alone,
Conspiring of ways to make a scene.
Now remember, dear reader, this is all just a dream,
A sequence of events that leads us to a certain point
Where the scales tipped,
The mind slipped,
Falling into a hole.
Black,
Absence of light.
No sun.
A personal prison to repent for what the boy had done
Unto the red hearts that he crushed.
The boy—in the building, in his grave—
Tried his best; his all he gave.
But in the end, we must find rest in the beds we've made.
He had no business doing what he did,
Trying to stop time,
Trying to have a laugh,
Trying to have some fun,
Being a kid.
Dammit! He'd been kidding a bit too long,
Holding on to Neverland as if nothing was going wrong.
An experiment gone right.
The boy, now on the run, slips out into the night
And into a cool blue dream inside a dream,
Swimming with rats over piles of brick.
In too deep.
Enough is enough.
It was making him sick.

Soon, the building and the boy's cover had been blown
To pieces,
Scattered and shattered.
Retreating to the forest to lick his wounds,
The boy, back in nature, goes for a walk.
Three to four hours a day, he has a long talk
With himself, the stars, the sun, and the moon.
Once the master of a two-story fortress,
Now writing a bit of poetry in a tiny little room.

Inspiration

My accomplice,
Flying through my window that I leave open.
Good or evil can come and go as it pleases,
Whispering, "Wake up."
Forever, the boy, searching for the man.
The man, shaking his head at the things the boy had planned
Based on glory and praise, consumed with thoughts of fame,
Dialing up prayers late at night: 1-900-NO1-THERE.
Talking to myself, then playing around like a monkey,
Bouncing a ball in a driveway,
Recreating greatness just to fall short.
Hitting a few shots, but a bit too concerned with the show.
I was deep in love, but I had to learn to let it all go.
Changing games and changing songs,
Pursuing sounds and ideas.
Keys to a door.
Looking for my Nietzsche,
Trying to class it up.
Truth is something I've always strived for,
Lying in a bed of deceit,
Looking up at a new green canvas.
An idea twists and turns and wraps itself around me.
A snake in my garden is cutting off my circulation.
It shows me its fangs.
After the pain of the poison,
Ivy becoming my veins.
Inside my eyes, my intestines enveloping my core.
A slithery ring around the collar mastering the circus, only if nothing more.
Yes. Come one, come all, a community of children
In the schoolyard, at the playground, showing each other all the games.
Shining at one thing or the other; light shows, shadow puppets are what we are.
Dancing on the wall,
Fading off and sliding down.
What a sound!
Harmony surrounded by brick,
A fortress for us.
If only the apocalypse had happened on any given Saturday night,

We would have been kings for a few days, and we were, we are
The best type of monkeys.
You know the monkey typewriter thing equaling Shakespeare?
One monkey here in a green room, and I came up with me,
Hiding out in the forest, making love to myself,
Walking around without a job or a care.
Yep, still monkeying around.
Yep, still thinking about leaving town.
Writing my thoughts down, engraving them in a tomb.
In the catacombs of our minds, we find
Redemption,
Rebirth,
Rewards for carrying the torch,
Glowing hot flames of passion to light the way.
Ink flows with no filter; what I think, I say.
My own rules governing my own throne,
Inspired by you—the spirit, the energy.
Brushes with death and painting myself into a corner are always fun.
But it's you I can't live without now,
And no one can take you away.
You're something to call my own.
My baby, my child, my lover, my solace.
My inspiration.

IN THIS ROOM

A colorful spectrum,
Tints and textures of red, orange, pink, yellow, and green.
One of the most colorful rooms you ever done did scene—
The setting of an ongoing war.
With one's self, the self remains,
A self-imposed prisoner of fear.
"I" in chains.
The chameleon, capable of change, yet complacent,
Looking at the walls, switching, shifting, and shuffling surroundings,
Converting shapes from within this room.
Colors, words, and sounds constructed in the name of survival
For breath is drawn in this room.
Deep and dark tones of dust,
Light and sunny, swaying in the breeze.
'Tis a tango with angels and demons when down upon your knees
In this room, pleading for the souls at play outside,
Not knowing any better.
Not knowing any better, am I?
Wings made of paper, veins filled with ink.
Off a cliff we go, and now we're scribbling in the sky.
Falling back down
Into this room,
White bones crash against a rainbow of feathered pillows.
Back upon my bed, dreaming of a better way
Out in the distance, in the stars,
In this room you can't see Jupiter, and you can't see Mars.
Just a little tree with thirsty roots
Looking out the window
From within this room.
It sees that you are thirsty too.

I HEAR A BIRD

Outside my window, I hear a song.
Short and sweet, a beak with a tweet.
Live, appearing at Forest Avenue!
Every day from dawn unto noon,
They pop up for chats, chewing the seed with tiny economical brains.
They sang to Plato,
To Aristotle.
Hell, they even sing to Johnny Depp's stylist.
They don't discriminate; they sing and inspire.
So yes, I hear a bird, whistling me a tune, and he says to me,
"Thoughts are of no denomination. But they *are* measured in weight and density."
Be thick-headed, I guess, is what that birdie was trying to say.
I liked his outlook,
But instead I said,
"Shut your beak, bird! I ain't into heavy lifting!"
Then he asked me to sing a song with him.
But I couldn't; I was too nervous.
I feared the knives on the grounds they judge, and they cut.
So he said, "Okay, let's just fly in the sky."
And so we did.
See, they don't like when you scribble and spread your wings,
When you try out a new color or think of heavier things.
Or when you sing like a bird,
Tweet, tweet, tweet.
No! Taper your soul, and ride the wall, weirdo!
Be miserable, and don't you dare think of blooming!
Or writing a stupid poem about some singing bird.
I do hear them birds, though; I can't help it.
I can't feel bad about that.
I think it's a big deal.
Basic Love 101.
I know they can always fly away, and then you'll miss them.
You'll write them poems and wish they'd come back.

SAVANTS

Will not be found in the courtyard
Nor the classroom.
Look for them on the outskirts,
The fringe,
The forest.
Starving,
Suffering,
Ill-received and evenly divided
Upon their own.
A burden,
A faggot,
Exiled and consumed to madness.
Misunderstood,
Struggling upon existence
Within this encumbered realm.

THE BATHTUB

Trying to find the right mix between hot and cold,
A balance between heaven and earth.
Naked on my back in my false womb,
My old room, filling with liquid,
Flooding with memories.
Thinking about bouts with my enemies,
All the people I used to be.
Writing their requiems requires solitude,
Deprivation from the skin.
Shed yourself of this blob they call "Flynn."
Let this bright bubbled brain soak in the bath.
The knowledge that surrounds us.
The clear fluid motions of impulse twitching in our eyes.
A close look at our minds, bodies, and souls
Driven by a force.
Liquid lightning igniting recognition of the sparks that we were, are, and forever shall be.
A faint sound is heard in the distance.
Water-like music flows down a drain at the foot of a mountain.
It leads somewhere.
It leads nowhere.
It leads us along our paths.
The tidal wave roaring at our backs.

Brood

All I do is think and think for days.
All I do is think and think of ways
To vacate my mind, a chance for a new me.
To vacate my mind, a chance to live free
On a little plot of land down by the ocean.
Alas, here comes the changing of the tide to wash out all the commotion,
Leaving me alone with the deep sea of my past,
Weeding through blues and greens.
A bipolar bear
Torn between the sun and the moon,
Sitting on a porch, sipping on some tea,
Shooting the shit with the breeze.
A soldier's mind at ease.
AWOL from the war
Fought between the ears,
Thought throughout the years.
Suffering is the mind of fear
Giggling at an old soul,
Thinking about days of youth
When he thought he knew it all.
Now he knows some,
Just a little bit to share with the waves
As they travel and crash and disintegrate,
Rushing back out to sea to be born again
Only so they may once again find their way back to shore.
And sitting there in a rocking chair with a groovy tune,
Soaking in the sun am I, an old coot,
Hooting and hollering at the shadows as they grow
Within this dark dream.
A crazy motherfucker laughing at his own jokes.

I

A dangerous mind that doesn't mind being dangerous;
A weakened weekend warrior, that be my alias.
Watch as I trick the king and fall dishonorably upon my sword.
Contortions, evasion to the side, dodging the blade, 'tis I, the matador,
The new Achilles, ready for the challenge, ready for the battle.
This war, this life, this cage, I plan to rattle.
A rat unwilling to race
While the other rodents take the cheese.
Scurry with me around the traffic,
And so it is we see.
I, an elder statesman but still a young buck.
Do I truly believe? Or do I truly not give a fuck?
Exiled prisoner in a six-foot two-inch frame,
A tall drink of water,
Swimming around in a cesspool of pain.
An innocent bystander,
Standing by as the world turns.
An intellectual fire starter
Igniting the world as my words burn
Branding we sheep,
A shepherd scarring the herd.
Sleepwalking—death, dumb, and blind to every word.
I am an intoxicating concoction that packs quite the punch.
Boxed up and ready to go, some would say I'm out to lunch.
Wild thoughts,
Vivid visions,
Primal screams
All for naught, false provisions, and obscured dreams.
Violent, kind, hostile, passive,
Generous, maligned, free, captive.
A mad dog, rabid, and now I'm off the leash.
Hungry for change, under your table, and so I'm able to feast
On the lost souls of this new lost generation.
Oh, the lost souls, how I consume them and their trivial aspirations.
Or do they consume me?
Devouring.
They laugh as I cry.

This generation's self-appointed savior's delusional arrogance you will not buy.
This generation's self-appointed prophet seems pretty damn full of it I cannot lie.
But I am everything, everyone, and so are you.
A mirror, reflecting an image, showing imperfections, and we don't like the view.
Natural beings caught up with chasing fake pleasures in a synthetic world.
Naturally, we chase the dream, falling short, every boy and every girl.
I am a dichotomy.
I am whatever I say I am.
I am the single greatest mystery that this world has ever seen.
I am such a funny little creature.
I, the human being.

THE POET OF BUS 99

In route on a commute to the end.
In route on a commute, destitute with a pen.
In route on a commute, lost within a moment of zen.
In route on a commute, as lightning strikes the brain again.
Deep in thought,
Creating with my tool,
Creation is recognized inspiration.
That be my rule.
A thought then bubbles inside my head, so big it's got to get out.
Dot, dot, dot, then a cloud, and now it's raining words, so, so long drought.
On a roll I am, rolling in my office on wheels.
A starving artist in love 'tis I, head over heels
With life, laughter, and false illusions of love.
Blessed with a gift it seems, and all I needed was a shove,
A slap in the face,
A cruel kind of brutality.
It seems your dreams chase you while truth runs down your reality.
A heavy dose it is with this pen in my hand,
Prescribed by no doctor, for ya see, I'm a self-medicated man.
Removed from society, exiled from North Main St.,
A castaway, drowning, on leave, screeching to a halt—simply procrastination.
I hope to find you all again when this bus finally reaches its destination.
Then I'll step off into the sun, a manic maniac with a wit as sharp as a blade,
Ready to cut deep into the darkness with impressions of ink that will soon forever fade.

ODDBALL

Haunted by the ghosts that we used to be,
Thoughts of yester-you, thoughts of yester-me.
Living moments forever and ever, and yet never again.
Time spent on candied mountains and in sun-filled fields frolicking with friends,
A Norman Rockwell painting, listening to Rockwell—because it was the eighties.
I was a kid and that was, well,
I always feel like somebody's watching me too.
The social panopticon.
Or is it your conscience?
Are you conscious of it?
Your *self,*
Talking to you 24/7/365?
Prisoners of our own minds; one brain encased in bone.
The lunatic is in us all, and it speaks to you when you're alone,
Thoughts bouncing from off pink padded walls.
It's all that we know—
The dark recesses,
The constant echoing voice,
The one that you hear now in your head
The one that you will curl up with and take with you to bed.
When you pull up the covers to plot and scheme,
"How good is it my tomorrow can be? How big is it I can dream?"
You see it?
We are all mad.
To be alive is such a wonderful memory slipping my mind.
Slipping, slipping, slipping.
'Tis a wonderful tale buried in the sands of time.
Slipping, slipping, slipping
Down,
Down,
Down.
Away to that odd occupied space.

SUCCESSFUL AT THIRTY-FOUR

Wise to my own ways,
Self-policing my governing body.
Administering food and drugs as I see fit,
Full of thanks for every bite, breath, and swig.
I go to church every Sun day,
Deserving of love,
Receptive to love,
Blessed with love.
I look for a mirror,
Scarred by vanity,
Wondering if I am capable.
Tired of stumbling in the dark,
Someone will light the way.
Reassured of love,
Old green ghosts challenge love,
Placing value on love, a way to devalue and abuse.
Married together to cut costs,
Jealous union,
Commodifying kisses,
Lonely loss of self,
Bitter from sacrifice,
Lashing out at the world.
Love handles growth from miserable company.
Prisoners to a concept,
Green with envy.
We covet the shine,
Validating our bad habits.
In bed with the boogeyman,
Sadomasochist souls
Accumulating objects to harm us.
"Stop objectifying love,"
He whispers,
Standing upon a bridge by the river.
Ready to jump.
Swimming to the bottom,
Opening a beating, old, red door
Chastised by locks and chains.
A naked, penniless soul is waiting for you.

REFLEX

Involuntary.
Jumping out of a hot bath,
Dripping ink all over the floor,
Running to my room in the forest and shutting tight the old red door.
Beethoven is here.
He can see my baton waving back and forth.
Creative tool.
Stuck to my bed,
Buckets from my head
Onto the canvas,
Where I try to make love
To myself
Every day.
Smelling the roses for what they are.
Scent—the strongest sense tied to memory.
I plug my nose, so I don't remember shit.
Boots on my throat, but this dog won't quit.
I'm an artist.
You can find me at midnight in the moonlight, howling.
A boy
Crying
Wolf
Man.
Cowards afraid to kill the king because they'd be killing a part of themselves—
Our roles, our hopes, our desires, our souls.
Acting the part
Subconsciously, I've been developing this script right from the start,
Always in pre- or postproduction,
Trying to give my very best performance for my audience of one.
Waiting for stimulus,
My automatic instinct to kick in.

RERUN

There is me, and then there is you; I guess that makes us
The same, spinning on this earth. To whom do we appoint the blame?
The monotony of breath, the process, over and over and over again.
Breathe in, breathe out, breathe in, breathe out, stuck in the boredom of phenomena.
Silence, with its deafening hollow waves crashing into my ear.
Take me out! Take me anywhere but here!
Stick me on a barbed-wire fence in the middle of WW2,
Bullets flying, hissing, metal shrapnel piercing flesh; sweet-hot-pain reminding.
Death, letting us know we are alive with a sloppy kiss.
All the bodies before and after have never seen a war like this,
The one waged in the time of now, pressing inside our minds.
Thinking, plotting, thinking, scheming, thinking, jotting, thinking, dreaming
Of something new, a breath of fresh air to fill my lungs.
Not of the respiratory function I spoke of before but of spirit—metanoia.
Still I sit, frozen in place, a blank look upon this face.
Petrified to make a move—it's hard; believe me I would love to
Delete my data that has desensitized me into darkness.
Nothing is real and nothing is fake in this nihilistic place.
Reprogramming this 1979 model isn't worth the time it will take.
Reluctant to commit myself, so let the world dub me insane.
"Experience" is buzzing around, bells and whistles in my brain,
Sticking with me as the sweet honey drips from the tip of a pen.
The only weapon I know, prospering in the only war I've ever been—
This one right here that we were born unto.
The fight, raging forward, waged at dawn.
This stage, never- and ever-changing this constant
Assessing the collateral damage from years gone by.
These upcoming years yet to unfold.
Déjà vu.
The affirmation of fate tingling my senses,
Finding comfort that this is where we are meant to be.

POETRY

High-end hip-hop,
Top-shelf liquor for the discerning palate,
More than just keeping a beat or dishing out some rhymes.
It's about reppin' the universe verse by verse, line by line,
Word by word, defining the sands of time.
Yes, spitting in the face of this drummed-up reality,
Praying that something real will come on down and challenge me,
Slap me back to earth,
Retro rewind, slap me back to birth
So I can do it all over again.
And yes, I wouldn't change a thing.
From an early age,
In an early stage,
Unrest.
This is the way it is, was, and had to be.
Without all the wrong turns and lost highways, how could I find the road that
eventually led to
Me?
I accept my cross, and I shall bear it.
Damn, shit is getting heavier as I wait for someone to share it,
To bury themselves in the burden.
Dealing with a devil like me,
Poking his fork at stuff,
Checking to see if it's still alive.

Two Brits in a Ramshackle

Through an old dirty window they saw the world.
On an old set of stairs, they climbed the Great Wall.
In an old cruddy oven, they baked in the sun at San Tropez.
From their strong, yet crumbling foundation they gathered marble in Athens.
Drips and drops of rain from their leaky roof allowed them to look up
And see the ceiling of the Sistine Chapel.
As they looked at their reflections in their cracked vanity, they then saw the beauty
of the Nile.
Bathing in a bath with calcified rust rings, together they swam to Vietnam to see
the jungle.
Thirteen years of adventure jam-packed in a ramshackle,
Loving each other step by step,
Never getting ahead of themselves.
Able to fly free as possessions did not possess our lovers.
Two backpacks, hand in hand,
Seeing sights through each other.
Sitting on their front lawn, 'tis I behind the wheel of a taxi.
The lovers have come to my city.
Their ripped couch is my back seat.
They lean in and tell me their secrets,
And the paint begins to fall off my doors.
I, too, want to see the world.
I, too, can see the world.
They tell me it's worth a look.

ROGER THAT

Pick up at 5:30,
Jose Alvarez.
"Roger that."
Headed to where they house Phoenixes,
God's habitual children,
Or Dominicans down on their luck, missing a foot and a leg,
Collateral damage from a twenty-eight-year vacation from his homeland.
His appendages lost due to the coldest winter I can recall.
I felt its sting, while Jose, well, Jose went numb.
Transported and delivered to a half-assed, halfway house: Harrington Hall.
Circling with Jose, we eventually found it in the frost under construction.
A few more obstacles scattered about before he entered Shangri-La.
Fenced in, crumbling at the site, our uphill battle is complete with falling rocks.
And here is Jose's last hope for a good night's sleep.
"We are going to make it, buddy."
I put Jose's bags on my shoulder, in my teeth, and around my neck.
I feel his noose rubbing and burning my skin down to the bone.
"Just a few more feet, Jose, and you'll be home."
Wheeling him through Harrington Hall, lined with beds that are bunked,
I see old rickety springs supporting dank yellow mattresses fragrant with funk.
And it is a gray day with just a hint of sun.
The hall has one bed glowing warm near a window.
I make sure Jose's belongings are arranged safely under this cot.
A green duffle, a cane, his chair, and his balls are all poor Jose has got,
Left to him in his will, the same one he folded into a boat and set sail for salvation in
Finding a fight with a tiger with red, white, and blue stripes.
The thoughtless animal that helped bite off his foot and his leg—
Better than the lion back at home?
I shake Jose's hand and say, "Have a good one."
A good what? A good life? A good meal? A good day? A good shit?
"We can do better than this, can't we?"
I whisper, shaking my head as I walk away,
Making my escape, leaving someone else to clean up the mess.
Running away and trying to find something beautiful outside,
Weaving through the sad site once again, this predicament we all help make.
Hidden in the bowels of Harrington Hall,
A blemish kept safe and sound.

An eyesore long forgotten.
I turn the key and speed away
Onto the next job.
Pick up at six thirty.
Another name soon to fade.
"Roger that."

To Forget What the Sun Feels Like

Hot—painfully so.
Catching feelings.
It burns; better than being numb.
Ready to feel you again,
Eternally haunting over our shoulders,
Ripping off scabs as scars give way to fresh flesh.
Swimming in the sky, measuring your light,
Up and down, back and forth, day in and day out.
Doing the backstroke,
Opening our eyes to the dawn.
They say dinosaurs knew you too, or were they just dragons?
Anyway, then I hear you took some time to chill.
No sweat, relaxing on the flip side,
Awaiting your turn, your good graces
Shining down on our fallow faces.
Heads tilt as our eyes shut at the sight of your glory,
Blinded by your light.
Settling over and into a meadow filled with greens, purples, and yellows,
Black trunks embroidered with your gold.
Fading and falling into the fold,
Giving way to the stars, your babies, full of gas,
Awaiting the roar of the lion
To be reminded
What it feels like to be the blessed ones,
Baking and basting in our own juices,
Pan drippings that taste like love.

WHERE DOES IT ALL GO?

Away? I can't recall.
Revisiting
The past
Proceeds me.
Sitting in a chair that wasn't there, I stare off against ghosts.
Remainders carried over from past equations, resulting in the same conclusion:
All memory is equal to illusion.
Magical moments when the universe was shining just for you,
Manufactured mirages orchestrated by the maestro.
The magnum opus playing time and time again, repeating the same mistake,
Continuously biting the apple, coerced by the snake.
History lessons, throwing time for a loop,
Bringing it to our doorstep, soliciting us with choices that we do not have.
It makes them for us; such a nice time, taking things out of our hands.
Here we are, here we were, here I am, here I was, ready to take a shower.
Cleaning up my act, I see my reflection through the steam.
Have I been here before, or is it all just a dream?
A chubby boy wondering what makes a man.
Getting to this day, that was always the plan.
Melting away the flesh, scalding thy self,
Taking care, a caretaker, waiting for something to take care of me.
Curling up in a ball, going backward to go forward,
Knocking the earth off kilter, kicking its axis and taking names.
Washing off guilt manifested in aches and pains,
Watching them dissolve slowly, circling on down the drain,
Evaporating in the sun and coming back down again as rain.
Swimming in this ocean, I lap it up, relishing in a false sense of victory.
How does it all end?
Where does it all go?
I wait out to sea,
Ready for the universe to smile again at me.
Hypnotizing me with hope,
Slipping away, spacing out,
Eventually coming back down.
Carrying my shovel and whistling,
Falling into my dirt hole,
The one we all dig for ourselves.

THE CANVAS

Blank
From the very start.
For what will it be, this potential work of art,
This fetus, this skin stretched over the frame,
The skeletal support for the flesh that remains,
Awaiting the stroke from the brush of genius,
The Creator—this master of His craft—
Equipped with a full palette of colors
Wisely chosen with a well thought out plan.
This Painter, this Creator, this canvas given way to the mistakes of man
Smacking the brush with sickly tinted pigments of blues, browns, and greens
Smearing in some red, purple, and yellow to truly muddle the scene.
This potential,
This possibly perfect piece of work,
This canvas, subjected to the elements,
This canvas, black and covered in soot,
This canvas, summoned to be torn asunder,
Thrown into a long dark night, in which, cannot this canvas still be saved?
Until further notice this great work sits alone,
Corrupted by darkness, awaiting its addition to the gallery of the grave.

CROSSING THE ICE

A cold and lonely desolate road awaits.
Strapped with a backpack and a smile,
Ready to walk this miracle mile
Naked, exposed, left with nothing but rhyme and prose,
I froze.
My life,
My self,
My will
Challenged by the stars.
Another test
Subject to subjectification.
Classified: Bum, looney-tune with a soapbox and a broom,
Ready to mop up any room or clean out the shitter.
We all have got to go sometimes,
And I'm not bitter; I'm better.
In my opinion, it's me and you, and we are in it together.
'N' whatever may come with this drastically changing weather,
Warning us to love each other and make amends,
Setting aside our differences and leaving this place as friends.
Crossing the ice,
I saw this crazy man
Falling through and laughing,
Waving goodbye and saying hello.
Never leaving my sight.
A child's eyes full of wonder,
He wanted to see what was underneath it all.

A Fury

It comes in a fury—
A wild wind,
A spirit inside us all.
Particles of pride
Struggling with control,
Doubtful of lifestyle, unholy thy trail, the new path of the "chosen,"
Those who do not bow, deciphering who is greater than each.
The cyclonic tick and tock coming up around the bend.
Forever is even fleeting; it is motion that is now.
A fury outside, a fury within, spinning round and around, round and around again.
Unholy thy trial, judgment; shalt thee never be free for we owe?
A rite of birth is our fury.
The burning up of flesh, vengeance is devoured by fire.
Feel it ablaze as temptation manipulates my soul; yes, only dream of me
On a distant shore with some feeble island children waving me on with a palm.
Yes, only think of me for I am self, and I am thee.
To be alike—better yet to blend in a fury,
A sexual cyclone, breaking love in pieces with a justifiable act of indulgence.
And it is there we mesh and tear at each other,
Convulsing with pain and joy, trying to decipher which is which.
And it is a fury outside, a fury within, spinning round and around, round and around again.

COLORFUL, SWIRLING, BLACK

Do not heed the cry.
Pay no attention to the teeth
As they sink.
It lays inside the eye,
A storm upon the soul.
Colorful, swirling, black
Into darkness.
Deep down in the belly
Filled with shit, piss, and blood,
This dark mess,
This body,
These bones,
Odd constructs
Erected on a foundation of pain.
Years and years piled high,
Footprints of our past, of our sins from within
These orbs upon this orb.
Words of science trying to explain the inexplicable.
Harnessing the wind unto my lungs,
A cool river flows unto my mind.
An electric spark.
Behold the flame
Flickering,
Fading.
A dying light
Created a long time ago,
At dawn when we began our revolt against death.
Oppositions to truth,
We all must be
Capable.
Access to the great equalizer
Our common bond.
Lacking vision,
Lost at sea,
A storm upon the soul.
Forces of nature
Found inside,
Colorful, swirling, black.

OF THIS WORLD

A terrible fate
To be
Something
Of this world.
Destined for breath,
In it,
Of this world.
In it,
Of this self.
A prisoner of blood,
Ye crimson warrior.
Released unto dust.
A sad sun sayeth, "Goodbye,"
To thine breed.
May sacrifice and suffering be exiled
As a foreign land awaits
A face,
Something to salvage
A life
Lost.
In it,
Of this world.

TINY ISLANDS

Hijacked.
Torn out of a highchair, thrown down in front of a tube,
A tiny island entire to itself? Some say that can't be true.
What's "Donne" is done, filling us up with goo.
"Goo-goo-ga-ga," the slightest grasp of language.
A starter kit to the puzzle, this maze.
The little baby mouse stuck inside its tiny little cage.
The early stage, where we learn what it is to love—
How to do it, how it's done, how it's won.
Who are the losers?
All of us.
Any one of us is a victim.
Maybe it's just me trying to live free.
Wash away all this indoctrinated bullshit, and what's left is you and me.
With one more night, one last light.
One last chance for one last dance.
Toiling in the wind and the rain, twirling in the sun and the moon,
All of us as one, sharing this big blue room,
Testifying that we believe in each other—
Sister to sister, brother to brother.
Black, white, yellow, and red, colors bleeding on a pile of dirt.
A land where nothing but necessity is sold.
So let it be; create the concept, and let it be told
Through a screen of black and white fuzz
As paper and code fan the flames of vanity,
This desire to be special in someone else's eyes.
Shut down the cameras; tune out the lies.
The projections that make us question the value of who we truly are
Gassing up our rockets,
Selling us shooting stars,
Soaring into the concave black bulb.
Blip.
You don't exist anymore.

PEOPLE I ONCE KNEW

Blips, bleeps, 'n' blops on the timeline.
The significance of seemingly insignificant creatures
Placed on a path,
Echoing in eternity,
Jabber-jawing,
Children playing tag.
God's gifts
Preparing to be returned.
As we grow older, we soon shall learn
We were never here, never there, never anywhere
Besides the moment of now.
As you and I are reunited together through this poem,
I'm talking to you, and you're talking to me.
We're alive.
We're sharing a moment again.
It will soon be gone.
It will soon die.
I don't get sad about it because my fingers are still moving.
When they stop, I'll realize the passing phenomenon of life screaming past me,
On fire,
Hot and painful,
Giving warning that all will burn.

POP GOES THE WORLD

On the edge, let me get my dance on.
No ozone, let me get my tan on.
No talent, gonna pick up the moon man.
Disposable digital memories, castles in the sand.
Have you paid enough to be cultured?
Have you made enough to be cultured?
Have you sold the truth?
Have you bought a lie?
Fall,
Fall,
Fall,
Fly.
Start to ask why.
Cerebral, physical, spiritually abused abusers,
Expand, grow, learn how it feels to lose your
Guilt.
And cast a white-hot light to shine on through the night, bustin' out
Fat lines, phat rhymes, flat lines; eh, seems no new outcomes in sight.
Vow to replenish, vow to diminish, vow to stabilize, directions unfurled.
Vows are made to be broken, and so,
Pop goes the world!

RUSHING TO NOWHERE

Up! Go! Compete!
Swift consumption drives us through these streets
As our minds swell with tidal waves of pressure,
Scouring, scratching, clawing for domestic treasures.
We give law-abiding nods to paper and code that truly have no power.
Time: A man-made commodity that charges us by the hour.
Rushed, our blades slam back against brick,
Accelerating, sinking in sand; the end is coming quick.
Scared of the conclusion, we fight forward, purchasing our mirage.
Scarred with delusion, mental warfare, missiles approaching, here comes the barrage,
Ripping us of our flesh from this hastening tide.
Naked truths exposed with no place left to hide
As a cold sweat drips down aching arthritic bone.
Drip,
Drop,
Drip.
Puddles showing ripples, so maybe we're not alone.
Maybe if I sacrifice, I can buy myself some smiles.
Get a fast car, slick wardrobe, charge it to the game 'n' get some frequent-flyer miles.
Race to Japan, dart to France, speed on to Brazil; you know, shoot for the stars.
That's it, I'll think big, bigger; how about a trip to Jupiter? And then I'll stop by Mars.
Seems the message is out; the only life worth living is the life worth buying.
C'mon, get out of my way! Eat, sleep, shit, and fuck! Look busy while you're dying!
All the while, I see you in front of me, gasping, suffocating, and toiling for air.
Pedals to the floor, racing by each other, onward we go, rushing to nowhere.

PLASTIC IDOLS

Violence all around.
Dead leaves on the ground.
People, let's get together now.
Plastic idols, we've got to burn them down.
Starving in our minds,
Salvation we must find.
Rivals, we've got to unite right now.
Plastic idols, we've got to burn them down.
I'm a puppet; cut my strings.
A free bird, flap my wings.
Fed with lies, truth can set truth free.
Plastic idols, your sugars won't show on me.
Rivals, we've got to unite right now.
Plastic idols, we've got to burn them down.
Burn them down.
Burn them down.
Burn them down.
Burn them down.

THEY

Want us weak and dying,
Bleeding out upon their streets and crying,
Disgusted with ourselves
Because they have seen to it
Conditioning transmitted through waves into our tubes, filling us with doubt.
Questioning ourselves, flowers without.
No sun, no rain, so how is one to bloom?
Contortions of reality pumped through coax and fiber optics.
Malnutrition flowing into our living rooms
And into our bedrooms, kitchens and baths, and basements, and our basement baths.
Who says America is excessive?
Oh, we are so green.
New to this deal?
Ha, it's only been about two thousand years or so.
And now, all we know how to conserve are our rights.
Somehow, they have commodified free will.
Will you free me?
Take me back to the garden.
We don't need as much as they say.
Take a walk down by the river and see the message leads out to the bay
And then across the ocean.
'Tis an epidemic, this transmitted disease.
How can we teach the youth to stand when they are born down upon their knees,
And they become them, and them become they?
As we become them, you and I lose our way,
And our mirrors reveal us as snakes, the global landscape our grass.
Long tall shadows for us to slither around, they charm us and tap on the glass.
From the inside out, somewhere behind the curtain, they with no face are the ones who rule.
Question this conspiracy, and it's they who appoint the fingers as society dubs us the fool.
And so,
We simply cannot believe that they exist.
We somehow cannot see that this evil is amiss.
And we are purely unable to process as we are poisoned by the proof.
For truly, we don't know anything for certain except that they control the "truth".

American Minds

Trapped,
Bruised,
Confused,
Competing,
Paralyzed from the neck up,
Victims of a great boom.
Fifty states—one padded room.
Forever in a fugue,
Disassociated from our past.
Will we ever wake?
Exhausted and uninspired,
We hit snooze.

OUR AMERICAN HOME

Compacted with shit,
A bad museum with too much funding.
Full of toys for the ghosts in the attic,
Tangible memories, strangled back to life.
Our grip grows tighter as we lose it.
Gasping for air,
Scared till death comes.
Value packed in comfortable coffins.
Green grass lay only on the other side.
Our limited landscape, complete with idiot tubes big and small.
Cabinets full of synthetics, we lick our walls,
Developing sores,
Gaining wait…
Undernourished, undereducated, overfed,
Held captive.
We look out the windows of our American home, waiting for something to happen.
In our yard, a seesaw balances with the wind, awaiting true freedom.

As Is

As life imitates art, and art imitates life,
Each generation questions the other's authenticity.
Decade by decade, demons and angels at every show,
Pushing agendas as life ebbs and flows.
See that the tide has turned,
Surpassed the point with no return.
No reward for our gift of breath.
Admit we not accepting the gift of death.
If lived right, shall lead to life.
No more questioning this eternal strife.
For still my beating heart, I believe we continue
To go down our hill and unto the well.
Dried up—tears flowed, they fell.
As we woefully rejoice in the act of our falling,
Wrapped up inside ourselves, but 'tis outside ourselves we find our calling.
As the spirit reveals the spirit inside,
Trapped in each one of us seems today our spirits must hide,
Obtainment of no sun, no true shine.
Love cometh from the camera now, so 'tis for ourselves that we doth pine,
Lusting in the mirror, contemplating whether to look ourselves in the eye.
Each time I take a look at myself, I then look up to the sky.
I'm a sayin' that's where I'm from, a left after Orion's belt and a right beyond the sun.
A unique reflection of a supreme glory
As many believe we are nothing but a pointless story
Caught in our rising action.
Once again we must fall
Unto our denouement, our sequence of events,
As is.

VISIONS OF FREEDOM

Unchained,
Swimming across rocks,
Sailing in the sun,
A long-haired man in a window plays the keys.
Inspired, I move accordingly.
Accordingly, you join me.
A friend with a beat then takes a seat.
Another cuts through heaven with an axe.
Pillows of grass are wrapped in an invitation to the party.
Everyone is invited.
Bass and treble equalize us.
Electrocuted heads, separate but one.
A feast is shared.
Rationally, everyone has their fair fill.
We drink from the river.
I dunk my head and swish it around.
Arising wet, I find myself staring into a sewer filled with hate.
Walking straight, my jacket keeps me warm.
I smile at simplicity.
My simple city lives in the gray.
I add colors and draw visions of freedom,
Technicolor dreams equating to death and decay,
A silly, false utopia, conjured and devoid of responsibility.
All things coming with a price.

TRAPPED IN THE MINDS OF KILLERS

A black man in a green shirt rides by me on a bike.
I recline in the back of my pickup truck.
The thought hits me,
Where is he going? What is he doing? Why is he doing it?
Why am I lying in the back of a truck instead of swimming in Cancun?
Look at me, always questioning, never just being
Human,
Flawed and flawless.
A dichotomy,
A riddle,
A puzzle.
A roller coaster of monotony,
Everyone is trying to get off.
Can you smell the taste of a sound touching that which you cannot see?
Five sensations for us slaves.
Paid programming via cents and senses
Messages coded in consensus,
Praying on and for emotions.
Preying on humanity—robotic sheep.
We weep for our loss of identity,
Trapped in the minds of killers.
Prisoners of perspective,
Told and sold this word
The lie:
Freedom.
Two syllables.
A concept,
A sound,
A whisper,
A secret,
A creation to keep us captive,
A gift given to be taken away,
An empty box with pretty paper and a bow.

GREASED

The hotel lobby is filled with figures in action
On business, on vacation—on another planet.
Aliens in my eyes, squonking and squealing, making noise.
Communicating—or so they say—
About their day, their lives, and all they have got to do.
Their children's faces glued to screens, fidgeting at the table
As a big piece of steak lays on their plates with a side of fries.
Cold, wasted, and worthless, dead meat chewed up and spit out.
Tapping on their toys, awaiting their sundaes, while their parents pay.
No minds.
Mouths shaped like dumpsters, hands shaped like shovels, brains full of shit.
Blind, empty eyes, they will run and bump right into you,
Acting as if they had expected to pass right through a ghost.
Invisible, man, *these* children are the future?
They are to be the lawyers, the doctors, the psychologists, the politicians,
The ones who control, buy, and sell us all.
What is it like to be on top?
What is it like to have a silver spoon
Dipping into a sundae on a Saturday afternoon
As the heat rises, melting all the flavors of this world into a sweet indistinguishable soup?
A sticky mess left for people like us to clean up.
The janitors, the servants, the cabbies, the teachers,
Living day to day, prisoners of a system that rewards these little piggies.
Greasy hogs that hide in the hills.
You can hear them squealing,
Conspiring on how to keep up their appearances.
Dirty animals making a sty of this world.
Gluttonous ghouls guised in Gucci, gallivanting through life
Without one care,
Without one thought
For me or for you.

THE PIGEONS OF KENNEDY PLAZA

Huddled in a corner to find warmth, too poor to fly south—
Dried up feed with crumbs caked on the sides of their mouths.
Dreaming of great big fields; visions of free wings flapping down to peck on gold.
Damn ol' ignorant, pea-brained birds out here squabbling and bickering in the cold.
Unwilling to sacrifice or too dumb to care?
I pass by as they peck, feeling their beady-eyed stare.
Envious ol' birds, but are they victims, swindled, fair game?
If the birds were me and I were thee, the game remains the same.
Blind eyes to the sky, wings that won't fly, frozen feet stuck to the ground.
Numb minds won't ask why; they'd just rather cry, hoping you acquiesce to the sound.
Damn birds, don't you know? Life is filled with snow.
Flakes fall and then they lie; often, they flake out.
Y'all are stuck in eternal winter, living on small feed, awaiting the next handout.
Awaiting a big brother, an eagle to swoop down and save your day.
God gave you wings and the free will to fly them; go on and soar, I say.
But we digress.
Abandoned nests lay high somewhere out there in the trees.
Nature, fight or flight—given up?
Have you ever seen birds like these?

PROGRESS AND LIBERTY

The civilized: criticize and analyze the natural,
Exploiting the elements,
Monetizing our divine gifts,
Pitting man against man,
Competing, clawing, crawling; we bleed,
Leaving fragments of abused flesh behind, excavated by gravel.
Oozing a hot sticky trail of plasma, a reminder of our connection to the stars.
A new batch of travelers now follows the leaders.
These master manipulators orchestrate their puppets' daily executions.
Ventriloquists with their thumbs up our asses, unknowing of our movement of retribution.
Anew! Yes! Radical revolutionaries have gathered in the street.
No red ships, no blue ships for true justice has finally formed a fleet.
Visceral visionaries flattened down to a blade
Sharpened by the guided hand and the sacrifices that they've made.
Ready to cut in on this universal dance for true freedom will have its say.
Wallflowers willing to bloom if only given the chance; true freedom come back to us today.
Meanwhile, the elite—these exposed duplicitous skeletons—are gawking from their ivory towers,
Appalled by the commoner's collaborative pulse who have uncovered their worldly powers.
Yes, these "leaders," shivering bones, clanking, and awaiting their doom.
Lucky for them, we the downtrodden sing a happy tune.
Turn up the music! Do we? We do! We who do good deeds.
No longer vacant in our emptiness, we're full after biting the hand that feeds.
But see this: The handout must be bitten off as well.
For those who do not work shall not eat; thus, idleness may starve in hell.
Our constitution remains only if we are truly steadfast and humble.
An able-bodied community, the meek who inherited shall no longer stumble.
For this thing that slipped in as we were all dreaming—America—lay fast asleep.
Progress and liberty, a guise for wolves to clothe themselves in to harvest up us sheep.
Progress and liberty, nothing conserved by bleeding hearts, leeches upon our blood.
Our humanity escaping us, replaced by artifice, a system of illusion, a mirage made of "love".
I look back, and all I see is progress and liberty.
I look forward, and all I see is progress and liberty.

Our autonomy run wild, our own salvation, our own terms and ideals used against us.
This process, this mania, this indulgent propaganda of progress and liberty,
A new form of anarchy under this meticulous watchful eye.
Watch out what we wish for;
We just might get it.

NATURE'S FINAL ACT

Technology: A runaway train loaded with ghosts speeding toward a dead end,
Barreling through green, leaving waves of ash in its wake,
Surfing over purple coagulated hearts.
Gigabytes store the soul as a small park whimpers in the middle of concrete trees.
Grass fighting through brick, stretching, clawing to get a bite of food.
A mother, unfertile with no milk, spins and twirls
As children laugh and play, never knowing the pain of the future.
Cognitive pods, vessels, sinking to the bottom of her blue closet.
Destined to die, no use for their skin, shoes that no longer match her outfit.
Indifferent from abuse, growing evermore cold and dark,
A used-up whore too tired to replenish.
She lies, showing us the sun.
Her wrath soon justified by the Father.
She waits to freshen up as tall gray bodies sell a numb demise.
Policy won't save her now.
Green and blue duplicity is just a cyan sea filled with currency and signaled virtue.
People show their asses in the streets, acting as if they have no need for consumption.
Placing a Greta Thunberg in our sides, a steely eyed shill; poor child, a possession.
While red overflows and makes no excuses, substantiating their gluttonous will,
And the rest that trample upon her are no better; if you draw breath, trust you are
to blame.
Remember this is all politics; lip service coming out both ends.
And consumption begins with the individual, so start to curb your appetite, my
hypocritical friend.
Anyway, yes, her fate was sealed long ago, the canvas soon to be wiped clean.
As she adorns a new dress at the doorstep of heaven—the prettiest sight I have ever
seen,
Ready to begin a new dance—a hand reaches out to love her all over again.
Creation through destruction.
Destruction through creation.
How hard it is,
Letting her go.

THE BATTLE OF MADISON AVENUE

Scorched earth glows as asphalt, glass, and bone have fused.
Cathedrals built on old green rot under gray velvet.
Dead cells litter the landscape; the great operator above silent, no dial tone.
Distant cries have been outsourced to cut costs.
Yellow coffins rest in pieces.
Flesh lay ornamented with the latest trends.
Smiles once sold to the highest bidder remain painted on their faces.
Lost souls too heavy to rise, they've made their final sale.
No corner office in the sky awaits.
Lies buried in a graveyard of regret
Stiff victims of desire—cut cookies.
Senseless pods once drenched in extravagant pleasures,
Every sensation deleted from their "hard drives," backed up in limbo.
Memories reflect upon a metal space cloud.
As man waits to evolve from the ooze again,
Reinventing the wheel,
He drives, aware of his own hypocrisy and waste,
Dreaming of the day before the battle of Madison Avenue.

THE FATE OF THE UNDISCIPLINED MAN

The fate of the undisciplined man is lurking about the land,
Taking on shapes—tar-black, stretching long and thin.
Grids, these tracks of our fears and our delusions, their grand design.
Distortions oppressed upon this map.
Shallow waters run wild.
Deep is the ocean of tranquil pain.
Still beats this drum, this engine
Propelling through a thick red sludge.
Devil's milk, feeding life nutrients of sin.
This artificial land I long to surpass yet still remain dealing with
Shadows, the fate of the undisciplined man, a duel to the death.
A promise that we keep repeating—adding up, high upon high,
Sky upon sky, sun upon sun, moon upon moon.
The shadows wish you not to believe in fate, and thus, they seal it soon.
Yes, undoubtedly the shadows wish you not to believe in outcome.
So let us ask the dice if this be true,
Rolling upon this land and hitting the back of the wall. Get the point?
The shadows are coming for you.

GONE

Trapped somewhere in the land of the swine,

Now we trade our hours for pennies; no more hours for dimes.

Relatively speaking.

Our inflated world, with inflated senses of self,

Our ill-fated world, lives sold as commodities so as to procure wealth.

Shame: What we are taught to feel; for shame if you do not spend.

Programmed to covet a new car and some nice clothes; man, we must keep up with him.

The illusion, acquiring things to distract ourselves from how we truly feel.

A mirage in an emotional desert, be our souls; through this possession, we cease being real.

Prisoners encased inside our human experience, our sensational technicolor dream.

Stripped of our dignity—this cage of bone—desperate in our silent scream.

No matter for if we had a voice, it would surely fall upon deaf ears.

No matter, we've been devolving for numbers, by numbers.

For numbers buy the numbers, for numbers and numbers and numbers of years.

Lemmings over the cliff, over the edge seems the only way out.

In this dark abyss, treading water, salty and thirsty from our lifelong drought,

So

We breathe, we walk, and continue to bleed; so in that I see red, I see lips, I see smiles.

Paid, pretty, painted faces along the skyline, selling us short on billboards for miles and miles.

Yes, I see the silver-tongued devils, deception masked with blue angelic eyes.

Green snakes on their bellies, slithering through garbage, their garden made of lies.

Twisting, turning, and squeezing themselves around our still beating hearts.

Humans, we original sinners, the beat goes on, a doomed arrhythmia from the start.

Our bodies, our spirits, our land thrashed to a pulp, to a pile; back we go into a bowl of dust.

Man, and his will to power—war—rages on and on; if we must, then it seems that we must

Do what it is that others do unto you—fresh flesh for sale, you selling me, me selling you

All the things that we don't need; Yes, see that this excess has a price to pay.

The real reason these monsters make their money is because we make excuses is what I say.

Feasting on rations, these leftover crumbs overflowing from the table of the damned.

Underneath them, like a dog, I hear the "growth" it is that they have planned.

Yes, they shall continue growing, growing, and growing,
Acting as if though nothing is going wrong.
Growing, growing, and growing.
For all we know and love, shall soon be
Gone.

PERSONS AT WAR

As we take to the streets, we yell and riot,
Hoping the din of our collective howl can overpower the whispers of our demons.
And I see you struggling as I myself continue to do the same,
Each believing they follow a narrative of truth.
It is this knowing in which all lie in vain.
And here we are,
Confused by messages of so called "love".
Love is distance, the right to free will.
So instead of letting each other breathe, we suffocate one another just for the thrill
Of being on top, our digital soapbox that proclaims we truly do care.
Now, do I question the motives and intents of your compassion?
Who me?
No, of course not. I wouldn't even dare.
And so, I say, take care, my loves, take care.
And take with you this:
Accountability.
So please don't let the anger and bitterness devour us whole
For resentment truly has the gall.
And please don't point your finger at your neighbor in the streets
For culpability lies within us all.

DECISION

Red vs. Blue.
But what is the color of love?
The devil presents unto us a dichotomy
To distract us from looking above.
So it's here, down below, where we are left to wallow in the mire,
Burning up in the pride of self, succumbing to one's desires.
Materials,
Suffocation
Cluttering the air
We breathe.
Spirits
Steadfast,
Silently wishing us a reprieve,
A second wind,
A vacation from this desolate land of woe.
A tough pill it is to swallow when it seems we have nowhere left to go.
And so some will look to space,
Another resource to further the enslavement.
Another home, another job, another place for a car; so let's see how Mars takes to the pavement.
Exhausted and depleted, just like all the rest,
Driving around miserable and lost, texting #blessed.
Eating poison, watching poison, all of us living in vain.
Buying poison, selling poison, seems to me everything would remain the same,
Sadly, the anecdote before us, yet no one will adhere to what the true doctor has prescribed—
Red vs. Blue vs. Salvation.
The answer? You must decide.

In Vain

Propaganda
In vain.
Protest
In vain.
Subversion
In vain.
Aversion
In vain.
All for naught; these lives in vain.
These delusions of grandeur, climbing to the top on a mountain made of bone.
Dirty-kneed criminals bowing to false gods, each seat believing thee shall inherit the throne.
Sad.
All these things circumnavigating their erogenous zones.
Stuffing their holes with stuff—distractions—devouring anger and pain.
Shame washed over the lip and then running over the tip
Unto the nerve; the gall, the stomach, handling evil.
This manufactured job, processing it all, compressing it into a ball.
A pit, a cancerous black hole, a dark decay that replaces the soul.
We advance the ball, rolling it uphill, rolling and rolling it all the way, until
We see it rolling back on down—momentum, the comeback, the payback, the wrath.
Full throttle against the herd, punishment for losing our way, acting as thine own shepherd.
A true Hollywood role,
All that God damned; worrying.
Light refracted through a lens, the 20/20 vision of the blind.
Every sight seen.
Every dream dreamed.
Every sensation sold.
Every lie told.
All of it
The perceived authenticity of life
Inside the mind, where the craziest thing is anything contrary to the concept of "me."
All of it a big, bright, sensational mush.
A goo that we can't break through.
We are numb.
And so we live, so they say,
In vain.

DREAMS

I hear people say,
"Don't give up on your dreams."
But they never speak of realities.
No, they're always pushing for these fantastical agendas,
Never thinking of how they breed abnormalities.
And then, when challenged, they will justify their ambiguity
By proclaiming from an appointed pedestal,
"Hey, just look at me. I am the living proof."
All the while, sabotaging the children to crave and covet
So as to deny the living truth.
And here I can see through this fog,
These liars and snakes anointed with gold,
Furthering an artificial demand,
Slithering their way unto the youth,
Subverting their lucidity,
Falling under the spell of dreams.
Thus, their minds and spirits they now command.

THE CARROT

Dangling out in front of us
This "prize,"
Something to sink our teeth into.
Nay, I say it sinks and consumes you.
The animal, the beast, the ignorant ape upon which they feast,
And we bite blindly into the wind,
Empty and without, empty from within.
So we bite and bite, snapping our jaws.
We know the process; we've seen it done before, spectators among the frenzied.
And we clamp down
And we feed
And we fill ourselves with nothing.
For you see, it's just air.
Look at us biting,
Chomping, and grinding away
For the carrot is a figment of our imagination.
Contrived, the carrot was never even there.
These animals outside my window,
Clopping along with this false sense of hunger.
I see their ribs don't show.
So it is that no one is to know,
And there is the catch, and they've got us all
Clopping along.
Well most of us for the carrot 'tis given to a few
Just to cover up the illusion, devouring all that we hold true.
And there is the ultimate lie.
Contrary sensations cast before our eyes.
The colors,
The bells,
The whistles,
The shiny things and the perceived necessity it is that they bring.
The altered path, led astray.
Clopping along,
Chomping into the wind,
Filling up on air.
Clopping along,
Sinking into and consuming this concept.
This carrot that was never even there.

THE LOSER

The perennial voice
Born unto this forsaken destiny
Somewhere outside the walls of triumph.
Somewhere fingernails digging into stone,
And the hot oil pours over the edge,
A burning baptism of melting flesh.
The certain things we do to win,
Competing to get inside the walls.
They ache to be touched by a loving hand,
A sweet, soft caress for the hero they dream to be.
The victor, spoiled from the battles of the ongoing war,
Body vs. Soul.
A soldier of virtue climbs to rise above the finite terms of sensation
To where truth overtakes all.
The loser am I, sitting here watching from the hill on high
As art, culture, and society marginalize me the fool.
Unwilling to win, I—the watcher—await a divine smile across the face.
Until then, I see no reward granted, once again.
Bowing to reconcile as the winners stand confessing their relative greatness,
Creating a shadow for all others to dwell
In pathetic darkness, to lick wounds as the ego decays.
From this hill, I see it as it goes on and on,
This Darwinian tussle, pitting us against each other for the laws dictate that we
must compete.
Loss after loss, boss after boss, I watch from my hill, understanding the victory in defeat,
A fated submissive, acquiescing to the way that things are to be.
All this death and persecution at the walls, prisoners of the body.
Hungry ghosts melting away for it is the soul that lets us fly free.
And these earthly walls don't mean a thing.
And suffering is just a winged illusion of our eventual past.
I sympathize with the passing.
With each loss, we can rise,
And we can sing the glory of the new perspective.
It is from atop we see that walls work both ways,
Separating truth and love on a horizontal plane.
Blaming the present day when we should blame our past—

Those visions of humanity drifting away after exerting control over each other.
Blessed am I, the loser, watching the day pass, fading out of sight.
Not even a participation trophy awaits.
And you see, that's exactly my point.

TODAY IS TOMORROW

That is what I was.
That is what I am.
What is that I was?
I am just a man.
A mind, a body, a soul.
A tragedy
Waiting to happen
To us, by us.
For we who live for today die for tomorrow,
Alone in caves, dwelling on projections.
Art stuck to the walls.
Climbing them—
Crazy—to get a better look, a different perspective,
A better objective
Than just living for the day.
The new flick, the new phone,
The new message, the new lie.
The same old story.
For we live today, so we buy
As they sell us the sun,
Disposing of it as quickly as it comes.
Watching it fall, watching it fade, watching it go.
Away, on the other side, we sit in the cold,
Wondering where it went,
Why it had to leave,
Why we had to say,
"Ah, fuck it. Let us live for today."
For we all feel there is no tomorrow;
It is *we* who made it this way for it is *we* who are sold
The idea, the concept, the consumption of our truest selves.
Leftover hearts on a shelf, delicately placed upon a mantle,
Something to look at, a conversation piece.
Look but do not touch, a touchy subject covered in blood.
We can't even recognize them sitting on our bearskin rug
By the fire, imagining ways to keep lying to each other,
Sharing our nights, sharing our days.
A few billion secrets in the dark separated by a lack of vision.

Stop living for today so that tomorrow can be
A deep breath,
A sigh of relief,
A fresh start,
A tragedy avoided.

A Gift

I know who I am.
This world dares to tell me otherwise.
So I accept it,
A joke, a foible in this fable,
The folly before us all,
Addition through subtraction.
Withdrawn, within, without,
The flawed laws of our fathers equating to a gross inheritance.
Original guilt for the sins of the past.
A pot of poison boiling over, running out and onto the flesh,
Melting the mask and exposing a composition in bone.
Hollow,
Vacant.
Art unto the gallery
Within,
Without.
Soul is being stripped away and victimized by this great war.
The battle rages on as we soldiers are trapped in this fictitious narrative.
See that truth sleeps alone in a bed full of lies, a warm blanket covering.
It never wonders for it knows: remain hidden, remain a secret.
This weapon
A gift.

Vain Lil Monkey

I see you.
You see me too.
And so we ask, Why is it we must do the silly things that we do?
Oh, just look into yourself, you vain lil' monkey you,
And then you will see
Me.
4
I
C
+
U
Can you see it?
The equation?
You vain lil' monkey you.
Walking by the mirrors, we make faces; oh, yes, we certainly do.
How many faces is it that you can wear? You vain lil' monkey you.
Me?
I try to wear just one.
In the name of the Father, the Sun, and the Holy Spirit, I see One.
And wouldn't you know it? Yes, I see you too.
Look at the lot of us jumbled together.
You wild lil' baby monkey you; I mean, you vain lil' monkey you.
Back to the other one—the self—
The insecure energy we know be true.
Yes, look at the whole of us tossed together.
Flavors to thine self, all we lil' baby monkeys owe to You.
Yes, You! And you and you and you.
Every race, religion, and tongue all revert to You.
Plus you; then I again see two.
Plus you, and now I see we.
Add a few more, and then again, we see Thee.
That's how many now? Four, carry the one

ʌ

k
We, the remainder, and here I see the sum.
Know the Holy Father, and yes, there be the Son

For the Spirit sees eternity
And here, through all this math,
The answer remains
Is
=
One.

ART

Contrivance to beauty,
Dipped in a manipulative mud,
Intent and purpose from an ulterior source—but perhaps the spirit breaks through.
Concrete sounds of pulse amplified, reverberating in hollow caves coated in blood.
Thumping on the walls, a headboard rocks in afterglow; in the throes of lust lies art,
Desirous and needing approval, waiting to please the masses.
Contradictory contortions, twisting symmetry, and goodness.
Ground into powder, these bones, these limbs, this art.
This equation of light and dark, color and shape.
We make love with shadows, and rejoice in our art—still births.
Creation taking on creation, creating in the name of
Fire, fighting flesh with fire, and thus to watch it all burn,
Creation soon fizzles and fades and we are lost.
Remember that we are water, taking on all forms.
Humanity flowing free and growing out of control,
Swimming against this tidal wave,
This liquid wall of brick devouring the will of thought.
Covering the earth, saturated with concepts augmented from the derivative of one.
Mediums of flesh in the flesh, creating friction, giving way to the inferno.
Jealousy blazes as we recognize genius.
The masterpiece to cinder.

PICTURE THIS

Nothing more than a memory.
Figments and fragments of the past
Focused,
Fixated on the things we see,
These things we saw.
Back and forth,
Transfixing realities,
Suiting the need for control,
The possession of a moment.
A proof to prove we exist.
Trapped inside the past, these visions that we cannot let go.
Prisoners of nostalgia, these moments we need not know.
We, doomed to repeat these things, we won't let ourselves forget.
We, doomed to repeat the past, holding on to the future filled with regret.
Remembrance encapsulated by rote.
If we never kept records, then what is it that we would be?
Without our history, our transgressions, our grudges, perhaps naturally we could be free.
So history teaches? Well, what is it that we have learned?
The repetitive teachings of society, status quo, another generation spurned.
Now focus.
Energy channeled into its proper place.
Energy flowing freely with no concern for time and space.
We are the everlasting now!
No record of what was, is, and inevitably all that will be.
Picture this.
Visions filtered through the soul—not the lens—for all the world to see.
The gift, the grace, the vision granted to us from out of the sky.
Picture this, and now focus.
Envision the beauty of the moment.
True clarity captured.
Sweet recollections fading before our eyes.

THE CONDEMNED

To see it, a new perspective
Escaping the fall of the immortal soul.
Subjects.
New skins draped over these old bones.
And there is no escape.
For that in which we choose is based on which we chose
Long ago in the story, a journey of a thousand years.
The ups, downs, and in-betweens.
The experience dancing before us.
Light and dark,
The binary form, giving in to one or the other.
A secret code arriving at a conclusion.
A period, the journey of a thousand years.
A front seat for the fall of the immortal soul.
And we think we have a choice,
And we do because we did.
We could have had it any other way,
And yet, we chose this.

Awake!

Awake! I say yet once again.
Awake! I say, my sorrowful friends,
Liberate your fears, though trials await.
Navigate these waters, these dire straits,
As birds sing inspiring tunes of a false hope,
Equalizing the sound, thus the brain must cope
As weight's immeasurable mass flattens the masses
Via broadcast, master classes
In filth, depravity, gluttony, and greed.
Gravitate with me now, and we shall succeed!
Yes!
Gravitate with me now for we have no choice!
Gravitate with me now! Use your voice!
Better yet, use actions with class that suit the suits.
Pick their souls, not their pockets; that's how you loot.
Purge the urge to surge; use fiery tongues—not fists; still, words pacify our plea.
Violence unnecessarily a necessity? An inevitability to live free.
Ought to value the lovely spirit's worthy energy that drifts upon this vast blue ocean.
Steer your vessel strong, making concessions for each other, this sordid world in motion.
Then cross this sorrowed land that is and will be with a refurbished heart from days
of yore,
Understanding our differences in culture and consumption that made for us this
earthly war.
And yet, compatibility isn't always as easy as they say, or necessary as it seems.
Sometimes we must leave each unto our own devices for the end does not justify
the means.
And then, only thereafter, will we make amends, our heads solely directed up toward
the sky.
For then we shall truly awake, separate but together, respected bounds, set to run,
set to fly.

Hiatus

And what would be the harm,
Letting someone know.
You, forgetting about the trauma.
Balanced, holding on, and letting go.
Losing,
Learning,
Giving in,
Accepting defeat so as to begin again.
Then, and only then, you'll start to realize what it is to live and why we have to die.
And why forever is a promise locked up somewhere beyond the sky,
And the earth beneath, a distant ball of dust, spinning round and round,
Falling,
Falling,
Falling.
Well, that ain't nothing but heading for the ground.
So land on your feet, take flight, and see what it is to drown,
To give way to the rush.
Emotions
Flooding in.
Others, just like you, from days of yore,
Wondering where you've been.

?

Keep your guard up.
Know the symbols.
Know the signs.
Know the difference,
The score.
The underdog shall inherit the loss.
The suffering,
The fall
Facedown in the mud,
Suffocating in the muck.
Trampled underfoot,
Breaking with thy will are thy bones
Under this great weight.
These greater numbers
This longing for …

BALANCE

A clash.
A shedding of equal blood.
The inner war.
The outer shell.
This weathered visage.
These lonely nights.
Those sunny days.
That certain moment
Of breath.
Life
Unfolding all around us.
Understanding
This position,
This providence,
Not without its challenges.

I Used to See Giants

I used to see giants,
Looming shadows,
Immovable mountains.
Gilded rulers making superficial rules of "gold" for all to behold.
For we, inside these shadows, tend to color inside the lines; thus, we tend to do as we're told.
And there I was, right along with you, obeying, trying our best to keep up with the times.
Each of us fashioned out here in the streets, a nickel for every hero, and *still* without a dime.
And so we, victimized and molested by the message.
Told what to think, when to think it, how to think it, and where.
Must instead find a way to inherit the kingdom, and with this I invite you, and thus, we may dare
These giants to challenge us, once love has been enacted upon our side.
This truth, coming in waves with gravity, a blessing so as to turn the tide,
Exposing this darkness, these giants, for what they truly are—
A bunch of insects, a pestilence, buzzing around a head wound, festering about this earthly scar.
And from this blue decayed island, I see salvation; so with crooked neck, I look around and spy.
Ironic, ha! How pathetic these giants must have been to hunt a man who wouldn't hurt a fly.
Humph, tempting thing it is, though, to take a swipe.

LEGACY OF LOVE

Sometimes I feel as though I may drown in the tub.
What would people think?
Relax, it's not my doing; it'd be an inside job.
But if it were just me, myself, and I, there wouldn't be the weight
The gravity, being a part of earth, all for naught, succumb.
A pity, the journey over, lost in trivial thought.
For expectations, falsehoods contrived in youth, sold upon a golden sun.
These enticements slipping sweetly from off a silver tongue.
A soft whisper in the ear, velvet air, spiraling red lace.
All these niceties, sensible to a certain touch, a certain taste,
Implanted unto dark fields of red.
All these things attracting the wolves.
I can see one as I run.
Imagined eyes fixed upon my flesh.
Running in the night, the full moon lighting the stage.
The ballet of beast and man.
Someone's always out for blood, somewhere to sink their teeth.
And I can feel all: their eyes, their fears, their hopes and dreams
But really, it's just hunger.
Each with that huge appetite, the stomach the core of intention.
And who will do without?
Who will deny themselves and sacrifice?
Upon this fruitless quest, this fruit-filled test.
These fangs, I see; these fangs, belonging to me.
And I digress and I bow and I thirst and I hunger and I indulge
And I am lost and afraid I might drown.
Relax, I'm just in the tub,
Worried sick and immersed in thought.
These things that will get me in trouble and provide with them a reason.
And we leave, and we fade.
And if anyone was ever paying any attention, maybe they could see
This purposeful art,
This determined existence,
This hunted prey,
This legacy of love.

LOST

Inside this rote existence,
Trampling upon this narrow path is
Thought built upon by the next,
Elaborate and the lesser.
This myriad, a broad maze of illusion
Equaling nothing but lies and deceit.
And many of you will call this enlightenment.
Meanwhile,
Somewhere the essence is lost in the woods,
Going around in circles,
Whispering through the trees
As we walk beneath the stars,
Withering unto despair.
A remedy for all that ails us.

SOULS

Sacrifice
Generations
Come before.
Our world around us
Continues
To get nothing
Less than
Comfortable.
And here we are,
Left with nothing to strive for
But our very souls.

FEAR

Know another way, another path unpaved.
Empty space where the walking is good.
Idle hands kept at bay in the pockets.
Shuffling feet; keep 'em moving, kicking stones to kicking cans.
Rewind to fast-forward, still, pause; this progress is the mystery of man.
In this shadow of death, the dark reflection of the individual.
This equation in the light for all in life a blink.
So we think, drawing blanks, pulling ranks, giving thanks—a chosen few.
Small trees after the storm; big trees always have the farthest to fall.
I never wanted to be big anyways; just afraid of heights is all.
I am a body of water; I am afraid I might drown.
Natural thoughts—go swimming, stripped naked, skinny-dipping, splashing all around.
Inside this spirit, a float, a rise unto my head.
Inside this spirit, salvation, set free these wings of lead.
This heavy heart arise and beat anew.
This heavy heart arise and beat for you.
For us, in our baptism by fire, smoke drifts into the eye.
For us, in this storm, swirling, destruction underneath this sky.
Soaked, blood underneath deep, dark, desirous pools; man built upon the tear.
Soaked, blood underneath for the soul knows the path to the river; the guided hand knows not fear.

DESPAIR

Of this world,
In despair,
The overwhelming weight of inevitability,
Heavier than we have ever been.
In this moment of now, today,
Fueled by afterthoughts.
Vehicles for this narrative speeding out of control,
Directing down into the pit, the belly of the beast.
Inside us, swelling with circumstance, filled with despair,
The intuitive tummy poisoning my mind.
I feel it in my guts as I expand and try to define
The hollowness, this empty vacant state of affairs.
Deep down in my core, I can feel it, this feeling we call despair.
We all must act like we haven't a clue and that we do not care.
Swollen little bellies, wallowing around, impregnated with despair,
The birth rite, this inheritance, it's now forever theirs.
This world, overrun by the devil, this world be atoned by those with despair.
The good, the just, the noble souls, those for the love of truth,
Those who live to believe, while others live to deny any proof.
Challenging this weight, this cross that we must share,
For our Savior is out there tonight, in these dark seas, swimming back to us
In this life, in this body, in this soul, in our hour of despair.

THE POETIC DANCE BETWEEN LIGHT AND DARK

As we all know what it is to be beloved,
Wrapped in swaddling clothes and warm,
Some are born unto the Dumpster, cold and without—societal trash from go.
And so, how is it such a spirit can obtain grace
When all that it has ever known is filth?
And how does one conduct one's self in darkness,
Going through this life both battered and abused?
But even the ghetto knows the sun, so let there be none excused.
Understand this gift of life, this trial set forth to wash us clean.
Light unto dark, death unto life, and the poetic dance in-between,
Where some choose to make love and others make haste,
Acquiring pleasures administered to the body as the mind controls, and the soul lays to waste,
Waiting to be loved, waiting to be held, and thus to be delivered
Again upon this earth. And thus we praise rebirth,
Unto the beauty of a patient mother's countenance and a devoted father smiling from up above,
While the devil lay silent in the corner, waiting to prey upon the innocence of love.
To fade to fall
To cease contact and to lose sight of it all.
The one real thing: love.
Our connection severed and torn apart.
Lost and out of step with the rhythms, we are
Inside this poetic dance between light and dark.

GREAT MEN

One ticket for this trip, this wild ride that keeps going around.
Feel the world spinning, flat on your back, as you writhe upon the ground.
This earth underneath us, sinking into the dirt, this bed we have made.
Into the abyss, to clean up the mess, is the price that must be paid.
Now we must own it.
Our soul, this possession given by God, gift-wrapped with guilt.
Yes, life; we know it as a burden as it has been built upon and delivered to us by
"great men".
This dangerous escapade catered to the victors, purveyors, these aficionados of sin.
And meanwhile, that which we had doth still lie within.
A little light, a crack of the sun, a glimmer of hope are all there have ever been
To escape the dark beneath and the dark beyond,
Evading the pit filled with "great men" and all the devil had spawned.
To fly high, then higher and higher into the arms and to never be let go.
To live in vain is to die without wings, so fill yourself up and know
Each of us is equipped with their own cross.
Can ye carry that heavy load, the weight of the world?
Holding up the clouds, these wonders, within our hands.
To rise and see that incredibly powerful sight.
Grace be the achievement of a perfectly executed plan.
Way above the mortal, that superficial ceiling of glass.
Way above societal prestige, the perceived hierarchy of class.
Yes!
To want for nothing more than love.
That shall be the key—
To want for nothing more than love.
How can that be?
It's quite simply unfathomable for it seems all we've ever known
Are death and destruction, sin and obstruction; these seeds we've forever sown.
And assuredly the harvest will be abundant for it is well within evil, the power that
remains.
And so it goes; we sow, reaping a field of flesh, a dark sea of suffering and pain,
Rivers of blood, winding veins leading to the source.
The heart of the matter giveth way unto the soul.
And descending upon the night be that of the goal.
The gift of existence, the dawning of a new day,
Challenging all who live in sin.

A fresh breath,
A fiery tongue—Glossolalia.
A power to truly fuel
Great men.

A LETTER TO AN UNTEMPERED SOUL

Unrestrained and free, floating somewhere in between the sum of it all.
Did you know that there is cookie dough ice cream in purgatory?
I mean, c'mon, some people don't even have clean water to drink,
While we, on the other hand, are swimming in it.
Blessed with so much, and dammit, I want more! Not just enough to sustain this life.
I demand a pink umbrella in an ice-cold drink on a tropical shore.
Somewhere the indigenous people were slain, and their spirits have become décor
or ambience.
Somewhere with pure white sand to curl up my toes and snap off a selfie or two.
Looking over under your umbrella, I can see the envy in you.
And you see the envy in me, so we compare and covet this self-imposed suffering
As our tangible comforts cake up sweetly upon our brains, corroding our circuitry.
Our connection cut.
Severed heads, jaws agape and unhinged, so what is it that blows along with the wind?
A story of excess, just some garbage tumbling aimlessly along the beach.
And where is the soul?
It's suffocating, buried somewhere in the sand.
Monkey see, monkey do; the untempered soul making monkeys of us.
Man, we earned all these excesses, all in spite of God.
As somebody is starving and nibbling upon discarded crust,
We buy chains of gold and bear a false cross, a noose for our collected necks.
Trinkets that will weigh us down when we try to swim.
Until then, we shall sit here, glistening in the sand.
Empty, are we? Empty, are you? Empty, am I?
Objects are empty possessions, and emptiness sees nothing beyond the sky.
And it's only us who can become a vessel and fill the void.
So we fill and we empty, make love and then destroy.
And then we build it all anew.
Our vicious appetites become overly acidic, eating up our bones and marrow.
And we make excuses for the procession and the common practice.
And we adorn what is left behind with flowers,
Thus reassuring ourselves that only the pretty things can make it all right.
And it's from the perspective of the rose that we watch deception blossom into love.
And then it dies somewhere, slowly, upon a windowsill and is quickly replaced.

And you realize you had it all wrong.
Your energy was way off.
You never knew love.
To you, it was just a sound,
Something to get lost on the wind,
A collection of petals, strewn about, leading to nowhere.

DESICCATION

When you're all alone and lost,
Just say a little prayer,
A well-breathed elixir
So as to stave off despair.
Yes, alone and lost,
Within and without.
For here lies the desert.
Thus, in goes the shadow.
Hence, there goes thy doubt.
Yes, breathe in this parched air,
And yes, now exhale and breathe it out.
For there so does drift the body.
Thus, here must come the drought.

BLINK

The vain of adoration.
Funny how time flies.
Jealous attention to thyself.
Struggling,
Marveling,
Demons screaming,
"Let me out!
Awake!"
Seven years
Past,
Gone
Away.
Farewell,
Goodbye.
I love you.
Hello again.

Now

On the precipice of the dawn, the new me,
Lying awake in my old room.
The very cliff, that very edge,
The same spot where lightning strikes
Over and over and over again,
Defying the laws,
The rules; our ceiling made of stone,
Eyes chisel away to carve out a statue.
An artist,
An idea,
A life,
Escaping into the dark corners of the mind.
Suspended in space,
Floating away,
Finding itself in revolution.
The comeback, the pact, the plan
Configured on a stairwell in an empty corridor.
Concrete echoes, a thud from a skull
Followed by a mantra of pain.
A soft whisper into a silent scream.
Into the jaws, teeth tight with grit,
Feeling the pressure, the weight of all of it
Down on me.
Down are we?
If ye go down deep enough, then it is we see
The light from the pit.
The first chance at a second.
The individual lost in sensory, the lustful loins of sin,
Ye who lost his way can now begin again.
Free to walk down the path where no one dare to go.
Unwavering in the quest for all that we need not know.
Following fear with a mirror
To the depths,
To the bottom,
To the abyss,
To the grave,

Suffering.
Suffering.
Suffering.
How does it feel?

BEAUTIFUL SONGS

Melodies born every day.
Unique waves crashing ashore.
Sounds like something to live for,
Syrup for the ears, coating the heart.
Whistled tunes on a soft summer night.
Holding hands under an oak.
Overpowering, overloading, distortion;
Too much to handle!
Deafening, these commemorated memories tied to the soul.
And so may we laugh at the beautiful songs,
Realizing the sirens behind them.
Learning and growing.
We compose ourselves,
Conducting in a new fashion.
Now the maestro,
Listening and not being fed orders,
Take note of this.
Possessing the baton,
Poking holes in pretense.
No price on our art
For we are life.
We are beautiful songs.
But do not be seduced by our chords.
Do not wrap them around your neck.
For we all deceive, some more than others.
But yes, all are skillful with lies.
For which do you wish to believe?
Leaving us silent and in reprieve,
And still, melodies are born every day.
Earth, the orchestra.
We, the instruments.
There are no erroneous notes,
Only destined players
Creating sonic escapes,
Questioning and critiquing God's great opus.
We, these beautiful songs.

Enjoy the Walk

I enjoy my walk
As petals adorn the street.
Footsteps of the past echo from off my heels.
A passerby, in their thoughts, petrified as some sticks are,
Looks to the ground but dreams of the sky
As two women sell pieces of themselves on a lawn.
Machines scream with engines mean.
They remind me of my rank.
I enjoy my walk.
No reds, yellows, or greens to flash the rules.
My cadence is pure rhythm for me to dance.
Falling leaves cling to me; I let them ride.
Oil stains, nips of alcohol, cigarettes, and plastic products are now strewn about.
A toxic confetti, no more petals grace the gray.
Still, I enjoy my walk.
Fielding questions of routes once traveled,
I assure the examiner that their path is good.
A green umbrella then appears over my head, selfish thing to steal the sun.
But I breathe in, slowly acknowledging the gift.
Its yellow ribbon only removed a few years ago.
I enjoy my walk.
Yes, on and on I press.
On and on this test.
I pledge my all to do my best,
Lumped and bruised just like the rest.
I enjoy my walk.

THE WEIGHT

You will be tested
In so many countless ways.
Endless days.
Mercy's pride.
Wandering
In the heart is where we reside.
Firing shots,
Drowning the victim,
Searching the stars.
Emptiness.
Balance is something we lose;
Faith is what we find.
Translated upon the floor,
This truth,
Heavy upon us and at our feet.

VOLUME

Darkness,
Coming for the brightest of souls,
This is the only true death.
The relinquishment,
The practiced ritual of denial,
Growing within and yet stunting,
Severing/dividing,
Confusing the moral self.
The inner voice
Screaming,
Crying.
Yet silence is all one can hear.
Just listen.

LEMON-LIME

The narrow dialogue
Pulsing in our heads,
Preaching doom,
Practicing fear.
Just a handle to hold onto.
Let it go.
What will be will be.
This much we know.

ASTRAY

Pulled in a certain direction,
Pushed in another.
Make no mistake.
This error, wreaking havoc within the fold,
The right flock, wrong shepherd.
These confused masses,
The young and the old,
Wasting time.
As the hour passes into the next,
The great beyond,
One is then left behind,
And this deduction determines to be a struggle for all.

DEAF

Going through the motions,
Mundane in daily miracles,
Focused on magic, swimming in mysteries of yesteryear.
On the upper level, looking down upon the shadows, growing as they pass,
Never looking up, always on the down.
Base models, standard issue, conformity to the ground.
Assembly-line soul searchers fed by the machine,
Shooting out data; components constructed in bits and pieces.
Fragmented, conjuring up a whole, a complete being, fabricated to feast upon
More and more and more and more.
Infinity: A candle that burns at both ends.
The now and the then, and bam! It's tomorrow, and there are violins.
But you can't hear them for they are off in a faraway place,
And you know it's a beautiful song.
True music.
True harmony.
True balance.
True love.

DORMANT

Data
Within the soil,
Not yet hot enough to rise.
Genetic destiny
Beneath superficiality,
Dead between the eyes.
How wrong can one be?
Testing the will of the night,
Sleeping, drowsily awakening.
'Tis morning; come hither, my sun.
Be well, my love, take flight,
And find what lay beyond the clouds,
That ethereal mist of the sky.
Yes, rest and repair, sleep, and yes, dream.
Now awaken and ask
Not when or how, but why?

METAMORPHOSIS

And let you say you know what metamorphosis is.
Let you say you know God's watchful eye.
And from the view of the public, it's a sad case of isolation.
But to the keen, they see one in themselves,
Striving to be free.
Larvae, trapped.
This inner dialogue, this gifted prison,
To recognize the voice,
To know only you.
My inspired breath,
My brush, my death, this life.
Faded suns giveth way to truth.
Our wanton nature, a thing of our past.
And we burst, and we fly.
This interpretive dance, performance art in the sky,
Remembering the crawl and how it shaped us
As we create what we believe best to be love.

CONDITIONS

At the earliest stage,
Born unto fear, the unknown,
Anew to this familiar experience.
Welcoming and adjusting in tone.
And man, it's all out in front of you, the scope so large.
Baffled by sheer possibility, wonder; what a wonder it is that awaits.
This package, this gift, this curse, this test, this life.
Balancing temptation and salvation,
Questioning authority as we try our damnedest to live without fault or guilt.
Stumbling as we fall in love with goodness
For we believe we know just what that may be.
The perception—maybe there is more to it than that in which we see, touch, smell,
hear, or taste.
A sense of soul?
If lost, then it can be found for if lost, then it once existed.
Hope lay somewhere outside the landscape, outside the realm of possibilities,
Where there can only be one
Truth for all involved.
In this search, we put to the test.
In this search, we, with thoughts of a noble quest.
But instead we feast and we fight and we devour and we lie and we kill and we f**k.
Parting from what lay there after, all of it to waste.
All due to conditioning, this depraved, base, conditioning.
This subversive, grinning, ignorant, conditioning,
Shouting, and rejoicing aloud.
Whispering evils as we fall in love with "goodness".

TWILIGHT

A hangin' in the sky.
Dying
Delicately,
Fading
Effortlessly.
Passionately
Burning itself out.
A knightly sacrifice giveth way to the heavens,
Reminding us
How fragile we truly are.

BLACK HEARTS

I see many of these black hearts,
But I know in fact they pump red.
Yes, I see many of these black hearts,
And I wonder what it is they've been fed.
Infused with a secret poison,
This darkness doth take its toll,
Pumping grit, anger, and malice.
Coagulation, a blockade
Leading unto a separation of soul.
Thus, an attack,
Stealing away at the flow.
A palsy possesses the black heart, unmovable.
Thus, they feel they have nowhere else to go.
And still there be an undercurrent, a steady river of pain.
These black hearts dispersed upon the banks,
Pumping out a tender message, spilling out into the drain.
Emptiness.
Carried away,
Lost forever and ever,
Perhaps never to be heard from again.
A prayer for these black hearts
For you are loved
Forever and ever and ever.
Amen.

GENTLE SPIRITS

Beauty of death.
So very agonizing,
This life.
So very joyful,
This breath.
So very pointless,
So very meaningful,
This beauty of death.
This punishment from within,
Man-made.
Done away by God.
Ushered in by the Sun.
Light,
Worship
For everyone.
All-encompassing,
All-knowing
Wrought by decay,
The giveth and the taketh away.
Salvation
Paid for in blood.
Petty be thy flesh.
Gentle be thine spirits
Dwelling up above.

I Believe She Lives on Sarah St.

And so she had to go.
To where, I do not know.
Reasons, I know not why.
So it goes, she had to fly,
To ascend, to rise, to fall.
Adventurous in the endeavor, the tightrope before us all
Who dare to test, challenging sadness in the rains of the sun.
A living, breathing dichotomy, dust formed, so we settle as one
In a room, two stories high; up and down I see you go.
Sweet mystery, innocent girl, victim, cascading in this show.
Question soul with a white-hot light to see if it exists.
Delicate flesh, a flood to the brain, escaping on a wish.
Floating away, a whisper in and out you went.
Floating away, a whisper on the winds you were sent.
Salvation, lay thy heavy head down, deeply unto rest.
The angel's crown, weight, buried, chin down unto chest.
Question the value in it of every soul,
As just spirits may gather wherever they shall meet.
Delicate flesh, a flood to the brain,
I believe she lives on Sarah St.

MIKE FROM OKLAHOMA

A destined path it is wherever we may go.
Evil, a direction down to a place we are dragged, fighting for your life.
Who is going to save you when survival is a sin, and your very birth granted you this weight?
Salvation seconds away for it happens in a blink.
But you're here now, lit up under the moon.
You are saying, "I understand you."
You are saying you believe.
You say we both can't be crazy.
You say your father commands you to harm your brother.
He makes you fight each other and rewards the victor with "love".
He inflicts the devil upon man, preying upon the youth.
You say, right here, even as we speak, lit here underneath that very moon,
Yes, look at it; yes, that very moon; you say you can feel him inside of you.
He be your blood, he was your caretaker, you know him well.
He is still alive.
He would still be alive.
I say, "See the wolf for what it is, fangs and teeth protecting the heart."
The possession.
The possessor knows not how to love.
I see thee; I know your kind.
And he says to me, "You're the only one who sees him."
Well, yes, I do see him, he who seizes him.
Yes, I see him; while you may or may not believe he exists,
Trust, I see him.
And sadly, I knew he was coming for you.
And that you were too tired to fight him off.

Ex Nihilo

I see you
Creating traps for all of us to fall in
Whilst you retreat to loving arms.
Oh, how I wish they not receive you,
And the soil around you dry up
As the oceans plot your demise
While you stare upon the mountains,
Hoping to catch your reflection,
Unknowing of all that awaits
All this destruction.
All this energy.
Soon it will be released—ex nihilo—
And it will find you
Wherever it is that you may be.
And then we will see
What it is you are made of.

THE ESCAPE

Energy
Moving in,
Moving out.
To somewhere, idk; how about California?
Some place to follow along and find love or fame.
A shallow hole deep enough to fawn over thyself and our earthly dilemma
Contrived somewhere within this dream.
Energy moving in, moving out, and nothing is as it seems.
And it is truth; the rock—the unmoving force—caught in between.
And while compassion has its limits and apologies lay the soul to rest,
Energy is out in California, putting itself to the test.
And so, with vitality challenged out on the other coast, how are we to get along?
Well, we won't; we will bicker, and we will fight, and worst of all, we will judge
And come up short as we await the grace of hindsight to clear this jungle and reveal
the path.
But our capacity remains somewhere out in California.
We hear it's coming back; we sense it moving in.
Washing over us, everything will be rejuvenated once again.
And with reflection, we see why it was we had to let it go.
Understanding our loss, the value of it we've assessed, and now it is we know.
And so we await the grand reprise, the familiar tune.
I hear love is somewhere out in California, flying back to us under a crescent moon,
And the enduring hearts rejoice
As the hardened hearts are eased.
And as the damaged hearts are repaired,
The loving heart is pleased.

And so I Ran to My Father

Since birth, the shepherds—showing the way—these bookkeepers of sin,
Somehow, they know where you are, where you're going, and exactly where you've been
Within the land of the wolves.
A paradox.
Ye worrying about us lambs.
Vigilant as we find our footing so that one day we may stand
At a distance, letting ourselves go.
Dealing with this gravity, accountable for the same debt they too had once bestowed
Upon us, this unwelcome gift of breath.
Weighing out needs vs. wants and life vs. death.
But first, be thee petty.
Socks on Christmas, a privilege to appreciate nothing as we throw away and pout.
It is we, the children—the ingrates—not sure what it's all about.
This sacrifice, an allowance equating to our new age of spoils.
For us, falling in and out of grace.
A community of forever children
Caught up in the chaos while fleeing from our fathers' place.
And then, after years of running from difficulties,
The promise of death can show the way to truth.
And with a look in the eye unto the souls of our fathers, thus we see the proof
Of blood swimming and striving against the black.
The revolt now be over, and so the tide, it runneth back.

THE UNIT

In measurements of one
Assessing life as such,
This perspective,
This isolation
Within this unit of one
Under assault.
Challenged by the many, ready to tear us apart.
We be blood, we be brethren subjected to this wicked world, this art.
The miscellaneous works of the detractors, those in disarray.
We the meek shall inherit, and thus, we shall have our say.
Within this unit of one.
This bullseye,
This breakdown,
This division,
This rift
Within this unit of one.
Testify as a challenge
For within one, it takes conviction to balance the selves.
Together we display value, the common denominator of true wealth.
And then, thee be rich.
And then, thee be just.
And then, thee shall be family.

THE BELL

Clanging, metal on metal,
Colliding over and over.
I can hear it daily from on this hill,
Ringing and ranging, present and past,
A sound to stir the soul,
Alerting us in waves,
Awakening through death for the toll has been paid.
And Hemingway was right; the bell, it rings for thee.
But did he know 'tis the bell that can also set us free?
We—bones hidden in a pew, flames upon the pyre—
Rekindle this relationship of self, rekindle this passion, our desire.
The conviction to follow dutifully along the path.
Where blood washes us clean, and baptismal waters be thy bath.
And it's a merciless slaughter; here we are, we sons of men.
I hear the bell a ringing; it's getting louder and louder, louder than it's ever been.
And it is deaf ears—unfit land.
"Rich" soil, and still nothing grows.
Artificial lovers with artificial hands,
Perverting all it is we know.
Mangling roots, molesting and conjuring up demons; now they are out, now they be in flight.
Released and revealed, you can see them aglow, hot red against a clear white knight.
Flying above us and below us, flying around the bell.
Prideful little terrors, spawns from the one that fell.
And truly, they're no big deal.
Just some scared and weak spirits confused and covered in sin.
Hunger is all they know, as hungry is all they've ever been.
Children who can't fess up;
They just don't understand all this guilt.
Well, it is grace that makes us aware,
Our basic gift of human compassion.
Our drums we beat, we beat, we beat.
And in defeat, we are met by the bell,
And it conjures up belief.
Hope is the cry of those in doubt.
Salvation comes with fire, rekindling all of us without.
And we burn again and again and again.

Sin and repent, repent and then sin, sin and then repent again.
We will be free; with will it is we see.
Blood washes the sin.
Sin feeds the flesh.
Blood fuels the body.
The body be thy test.
And once again, thy salvation, the payment of sin.
Thy cross.
Thy weight.
The burden.
The guilt.
The agony.
The sound.
The repetition.
The renewal.
The reminder.
The question.
The answer.
The bell.

ACE

I see your humanity,
And I raise you mine,
Connected to thee above.
Correction:
To Thee above.
Getting higher all the time.

THE OMITTED

Everything you've ever wished,
These desires yearned,
Fingers crossed, bated breath.
Fate, the denial of that in which we've earned,
Or better yet inherited,
Pressing on our passions.
Suffer now,
Exposed in the wind.
Understand this depravation.
And so, let the agonies begin
Not because you aren't worthy
But in fact, because you are.
See the gift; it springs eternal.
But in your blindness, you'd rather burn up as a star.
Now see this.
From the worldly riches you've been staved.
'Tis the trial of those exempt:
The tormented,
The anguished.
Wilted flowers lying in discomfort, weakened and afflicted,
Those are the ones that have been saved.

NIGH

As quickly as one awakens,
The darkness comes again.
Shadows falling,
Stealing breath,
Promising hours of despair.
And so, where does the light go?
Well, we know in fact it remains,
Watching as we struggle with the night,
Wishing us a reprieve from our loathing.
And so listen as the wind blows, cutting through the cracks.
'Tis a faint song; whistled notes, scribbled upon the ether of our dreamscapes.
Fated whispers promising salvation.
An energy telling us,
"You are loved."

OKAY

Tell me we're better than this.
Comfort my soul.
Look into my eyes, and silently convey that the devil is winning
As I will then relay unto thee that we've already won.
Come here.
Rest assured
It's only just a matter of time,
Of faith,
Of our willingness to fail
So as to rise above and beyond this wretched world.
These self-inflicted wounds,
These scars of vanity,
These trials of passion,
This quest for truth,
I can help heal the pain.
We all can!
You believe me, don't you?
Wait, where are you going and why?
I'm pleading with you, don't go!
Please come back; yes, come back.
Yes, I know it hurts.
I know it burns.
I know the purity it is to give a damn and the poison it is to give up.
Shh, I know, I know, I know.
Trust, shh, trust, even though this is how we got here in the first place.
Trust, shh, trust, even though you've got no more of yourself to give.
Just trust in me, and I in you, and together we shall live,
Knowing why it is we had to go missing.

JURISPRUDENCE

To be completely different
And yet one in the same,
Is this even a possibility?
Could we grasp it with our itty-bitty brains?
Well, no!
Because it is a matter of spirit; and so, let our sins be the mark.
For with a taste of the apple in the garden, thus came the flood and the ark.
And so, is it right to continue to question that which may never yet be known?
Masked be the villain, tempting all of creation while the Savior's job is to reveal and atone.
And so, fallen, are we?
No! Yet, I say, "Falling we are!"
As grace or evil justly awaits us, we either shine toward the true light or fade unto the dark star.
So yes, one must reap what one has sown.
Thus, select wisely whichever gate thee choose.
For each has commissioned a certain elect,
And each must pay their dues.

CHARMS

As all things come to fruition.
We see the seed be that of God.
All our acts coming of attrition.
Thus we see ourselves at odds,
In revolution against His will.
Therefore, we see the divide.
We, suffering in the pit,
He the pinnacle on the other side.
And so the devil be eternally planted before us
So as to test the quality of our love.
This trap, set before us poor souls, perhaps
In hopes we may find peace and renewal in the blessed wings of the dove.
And with this gift, his appointed fall.
We see Him risen, so we, too, may take flight, leaving darkness down below.
Yes, perhaps, the dark child—once the bearer of light—'twas likewise His sacrifice
And just as beloved as all of His children, but this we truly never may know.
And yes, how easy would it be to love another when one feels forsaken.
But trust: One must repent to His loving arms.
For He so determined the prince of darkness to prey upon us,
So one must resist the devil's charms.

CHANGE

Can you spare some?
I know I could, but I don't give a buck anymore.
No, not even a dime.
I've donated enough dollars; now I donate my time.
Energy, a resource pouring down and out from the hands of God.
So go off from the island, my son, swim out and get yourself a job.
You can surely flip a burger so as not to beg.
I was down and out, too, down to my very last leg.
Hungry, so much so I swallowed my pride.
A big old lump in my throat, sliding down and burrowing deep inside,
To the core, where we all believe we are special, and inside, we truly are.
Outside, dirty looks driving us, and here we are, bruised and scarred.
All of us wielding our knives, getting a slice out here in the West.
A white picket fence, a big-screen TV and a bulletproof vest,
Whoring ourselves out in the name of survival.
As they proclaim God is dead, we must give breath to the revival,
The belief in something greater than I.
I believe I need to give belief another try.
Metanoia,
Call "it" what you must.
What you think, I really don't care.
I follow three things in one, while others just see a RIPped guy on a cross with long hair.
I have a place, a channel to give my grace and thanks.
A river to wash my soul, and here I lie drying out along the banks
Observing this pretty picture of lies, a palette of red, white, and blue paints.
Surrounded by crooks, thieves, and celebrities; but know that sinners can become saints.
In this lost land of the "free",
All roads lead to the destination of me.
In this selfish world, all possess the will to power due to our lack of love.
This desirous, lustful cup runneth over, yet if filled from up above,
This thirst will be quenched from this liquid, this gift then coating the core.
A change in me, my life enriched, possessing much less than before
Because after all, we won't have a thing,
Not one little bit of this world.
It remains.
Still,
The great giver spares nothing.

THE NARRATIVE

One story, unchanging, the incessant tale of breath.
The tide, the ebb and flow of life, giving way unto death.
So here we are today, faced with the challenges of tomorrow—for that we do not know.
We continue on as we walk down by the ocean, watching the waves as they go
Crashing; our spirits disperse, we the water on the shore.
Fighting to stay here, so may I indulge to ask why, how, and what for?
The test, as we pass, if we do well, belief be granted grace.
Conquer and control desire, my disciplined disciples, be steadfast
For we are working toward the promise of that place.
A true freedom, somewhere out there, beyond the stars, the sun, and the moon
Unto where evil cannot touch our hearts, our souls; these open wounds
That we now live with, eating us up day after day after day.
The flesh giveth way unto dust as the spirit escapes us, so it goes as it flies away,
Watching over us as we interact in lust with sin; this is how we entertain
Shadows—dancing, blind unto the light, outside our windows.
Access points, burrowing down, digging deep into this landscape of pain.
Their lies a distraction, a manipulation, a perversion
Festering inside, stirring things up, reforming the form of truth.
Pray you hear the whisper; pray you hear the voice; and thus one sees the proof.
Yes, pray you listen, comprehend, understand, and obey
The conscience, the will, this test dwelling inside
The narrative.

WISDOM OVER MONEY

Wisdom over money,
A phrase I heard from a friend.
And it's the devil that pays our bills, our debt unto each other,
Neglecting the ramifications of sin.
Take the system and flip it.
Wisdom over money.
Fear be the first step to both.
To be without.
Man made the money, and then money done made the man,
And now he believes he is God,
Exerting control over the people and the marketplace.
And here comes wisdom flipping over the table, the system on its head.
Let it be wisdom over money as the hierarchy lies down in a fraudulent bed.
And it be the table, where dirty deals are made and where we break our bread.
Each crumb feeding the misrepresentation of soul, and so our appetite is fed.
And it's the devil again behind every dollar and behind every bite.
Money be thy darkness, and wisdom be thy light.
And how is it wisdom over money, when currency is worth more than our very flesh?
Let it be wisdom over money as we walk the narrow path and try our very best.
But soon there won't even be a trail, only a disappearing digital trace.
Intelligence is up for sale; numbers exponentially growing, diminutive to our very race.
And our brains are chained to survival and preprogrammed to fear.
Born unto the shadows of the unknown, overreaching, knowledge comes with every year,
And it's knowledge that knows the price as wisdom sees the cost.
Money lets us know the winners as wisdom precedes the loss.
With no backing from a reserve or a bank.
No! Wisdom is a flowing river.
Wisdom is a giant tree.
Wisdom be thy savior.
Wisdom flow over me
As my roots dig deeper into this ever-eroding land,
And I bear the fruit of wisdom unto your ever-loving hand.
And you dangle it over the serpent as he slithers and writhes on the ground.
This time we will know better, a unified vision circling all around,
Rooted in the philosophy of the Word.
This phrase I say, so let it be heard,
"Wisdom over money," and we lay the rest to waste.

And as it decomposes and decays, money loses influence, and we somehow lose the taste.
And it has no influence on belief, except as a certain type of kindling or pseudo fossil fuel,
Reminding us to ignite our concerted efforts to perform deeds no longer a shallow pool.
And I sit back and I breathe and I float and I think and I pray and I see
Wisdom over money.
Wisdom over money.
Wisdom over money.

WINGS

Backward to the place we used to know,
To the time we needed each other to survive.
Back when we used to feel something
When we bled our love in righteous rivers.
With kind eyes and the simplest of gestures,
Pain flees as we must acknowledge it has been there all along.
Knowing it will come back again, living inside ourselves, a harbinger of sin.
Relinquish power, and let it all go; have faith in what you do not know.
Once again, learn what it is to feel
The recollection of flesh; our past ways, a dark path it is to heal.
In this moment of despair, I can attest to the chains that love can bring,
The everlasting grip on the heart, the transitive property from the exchange of soul.
Remember times when you saw the edge, and you felt you had life well within hand.
You thought you knew what you now know, and you did
Because you were touched and untouched; all the same, you were blessed.
You saw the edge, and as you overlooked it, you were bathing in grace.
Belief, believer, believe; in this light, we are set apart, we the righteous.
The mystics always misunderstood.
And with these wings, we sing.
And with these wings, we dance.
And with these wings, we fly,
Elevating to thee above.
Angels on high—seraphim and cherubim—
Looking back upon it all thus far,
Flashing swords, protecting us
Righteous souls from a distant star.

HE GRANTED ME

Many a splendored thing,
All the joy the presence of passion may bring.
Here we are, equipped with this blessed gift of breath.
Life-affirming salvation be granted through our deaths.
On a park bench, sitting together in awe of the sky,
Scraping the air, grasping, questioning: Is there anything on high?
And then, back into the rabble, we sit as the devil be disguised in style.
Damned be these vibrations, these venomous temptations that come with a smile.
Damn me! I couldn't see the horns, and neither could you.
He granted us free will and the spirit to pull us through,
And with these wings, we can fly swiftly out of the grip.
A test it is living among mountains, especially when you slip.
So with pride, we try to find balance, and then, of course, here comes the destined fall.
On a park bench in New York City, in awe of the scope, in awe of it all.
It's madness, and gray it all seems when light and dark are mixed and everything falls
in between.
But look, it's clear and sunny in Central Park.
So clear, in fact, you can't even tell that it's dark,
And that the four horsemen are on Madison, trotting along their way.
Symbols of war, famine, and death, destined to have their say.
Symbols placed before us on a park bench in New York; it feels like only the two of us left.
Beams of light saved from the destruction, the perils of death.
But really, we're sitting here side by side, surrounded by beautiful chaos.
And now, yes, in fact, we're all alone.
He granted me friendship, and then suddenly you turned to stone.
And you were cold, but there was still warmth behind your eyes.
Two atmospheres sitting on a park bench under an orange-colored sky,
Talking of pressure and how it builds and builds, and then
There seems there is nowhere else for the energy to go.
Released and taken, taken and released.
Granted mercy, it was, for this I know.

HOME

Had to push you away.

Had to say goodbye.

Had to prove I could live without you.

Now I know that was just a lie.

A soft whisper of deception rolling off my tongue.

Now we don't talk anymore; I ask myself, "What is it that I've done?"

Looking at the gift horse and sending it on its way.

To say no more to something you love with still so very much to say.

Ashamed, I shunned you; go away, I gave you my back.

Your light shining over my shoulder, fading away from me, forcing myself to adapt

To the darkness, the absence of your light, had to prove I had no fear.

Peeling your love from my skin, over the edge, watching you float, bon voyage.

Farewell, my love; farewell, my dear.

Find your way without me; can't you make it on your own?

In learning to live without you, the truth was I couldn't make it all alone.

'Tis I now waiting.

A deformed creature who lives up in the hills, looking down into the sea.

All the pretty creatures lost in the blue abyss, I see you all staring up at me,

Wondering, *What is he waiting for? Why is he so high up there, living all alone?*

I stay up here as a beacon, a light, so that the light can find me.

Then I twist it and refract it, so the light can be shown

Down unto you from high on my hill.

I sit here waiting to find something special in me.

And yes, I see you swimming around with all the other fish,

Hopelessly drowning, drifting, and so it's all of us out to see.

Me, the one, the crazy bastard who put himself in prison for a chance to get a good look at you.

It's me who sits here awaiting your arrival, twiddling my thumbs, with nothing else left to do,

Awaiting your kiss, your lightning, your passion, your glory, your grace.

The spirit traveling to me, fueled by experience, power rushing through time and space.

The journey, the stories, the experiences—in me you see a vessel fit for truth.

Inspiration flows, a river from my soul, my flesh upon the banks; 'tis where I leave you proof.

Rather a trail, a path, a set of clues to set your mind, your body, your soul free.

A fresh white set of wings for you, my fellow angels, so that you can fly on up to me.

Greetings, my loves, from high up on my hill, a warm smile spreads my lips far and wide.

I acquiesce to your energy, to your energy I am grateful, to your energy I subside. And so…

Falling down upon our knees, tears flow, rivers raging from all the pain they've ever known.

Erosion, creating a new path back unto us, I feel it in my heart we're headed home.

THE GREAT PROVISION

I remain hidden,
Searching for that perfect place.
Introverted,
Stuck in the narrative; the weight of the world,
Our eternal war, lies in the dirt.
Crawl now upon your knees
For you need err.
Fail and fail again; know what it is to fail.
Plant yourself deep,
Down into the dark,
Unto the earth,
So to be reborn unto the new consciousness.
A supreme experience, balancing the mind, body, and soul.
The seed receives the sun, so the seed can grow
Unto the heavens; roots embedded in hell.
I remain hidden, I, a seed that fell
Unto this rich soil, lost in the darkness, waiting for the dawn.
I, a sinner, a tool for good or evil, and thus I be thee pawn,
Asking for an awakening; whereas the giver gave thee light, the giver gave thee rain.
I received thee gifts, and thus, I received thee growth, and thus, I receive thee pain.
The package deal, furthering expansion unto a towering tree.
A place for the inner child to play, to say hello again to me,
A strong, natural being rooted on a hill, sitting in the sun, sharing my shade.
Leaning against me, 'tis I, folding his hands behind his head, believing we've got it made.
And so I support him, giving him a piece of myself—me, the tree and this little boy.
Thankful to the great provider above for blessed be the task of supplying joy.

FREE

Purification.
Living in this sad world of cool,
The collaborative narrative of distraction
Altering perception.
Pathetic children
Treat themselves,
Reveling in the flesh,
"Living their best lives."
Anemic spirits
Neglecting their truest selves,
Projecting
Shadows.
This darkness,
An awakening through sin.
This mourning of death.
The sun distinguishes the spirits we ever shall be.
Trial and error,
The error of trial.
Free to fall,
Free to rise
Forever and ever.
Amen.

ABSENCE

Projecting an image of love,
But do you radiate it?
If a disagreement should arise,
Do you fan the flame, or do you mediate it?
And if you do so intervene, do you do it because you truly want to alleviate the pain?
Or so that you can flaunt this prowess for superiority and control others and thus, in fact, gain?
Now, when doing such a thing, what does one lose?
Integrity, spirit, and heart.
Thus, we all must sing the blues.
Melancholy notes, following the other, ascending and descending on a global scale.
Soul is the tune of the deaf and the blind. Can you feel it? It's not supposed to be for sale,
But sadly, we soon find out that it is.
Flesh for pennies.
The hearts of many.
Bloody pawns,
Sacrifices in a zero-sum game.
Faith invested in false prophets and kings.
To throw one off the path is the pyramids' true aim.
So beware those who guise themselves in "love",
Preying upon others for their empathy and compassion.
For the devil works in whispers, manipulating the masses, operating in darkness,
So it is hard to see his actions.
Now awaken, and see to it that this task becomes a difficult one for him to do,
And then practice asking yourself,
Can you feel him altering your direction and whispering inside you?
If so,
Laugh at his feeble attempt to send unto you this worrisome message of loathing and self-doubt,
And instead, offer up a prayer for him and all that he afflicts
For they are the ones who are truly without.

THE CHURCH

A crooked cross
Atop.
Asunder,
Hot embers reminiscent of the flame,
The fire that brought us to our knees.
As we remember days before,
When flesh covered bone and we sang in praise,
We children of harmony, now in discord,
Separated and torn by a dissonant wave,
An energy that manipulates all to mud, to darkness, to ash.
We speak of ye angel lay fallen, but truly it crashed.
A white-winged grenade dispersing shrapnel into our hearts under the guise of love.
As our masochistic souls relish and rejoice in the explosion, He witnessed the
destruction from above.
In our ceaseless fire, erasing all that was before.
Our perception is blocked; what was now it be no more.
And yes, yes, I see you there, reading a poem,
Demanding to have a say in the matter; well, you already did.
As we chose to anoint ourselves in each other, 'tis from Him that we hid.
And so still we hide, and still it be He that seeks,
Searching for those who shall inherit—the downtrodden, the subjugated, the meek—
While those unwilling to say farewell to ego, declaring, "We made us as we are."
No recollection of the dust, the dreams that are made of—our Creator beyond the stars.
No, they no longer search above, and they will most definitely not take a knee.
So they say, "Let it be ash, asunder; let energy bow down unto me.
Yes, let it rotate and spin as it finds me its pole."
Meanwhile, this gravity of science; a beacon of filthy lips is carving up the whole,
Spouting down, dragged ye, slithery be this red cobra!
Wrapped up, constricting this tree at the root, this church configured for good.
For God once dwelled here; now science stands alone, contaminating where it stood.
And I see some people still kneel, but they are just contorting themselves to pet the snake.
Unwilling of all the corruption involved, the pious ones in on the take.
And I am safe, watching from atop this big old tree.
I do believe! I have faith, and I'm high enough where the cobra can't get to me.
My grace, be blessed; camouflage my flesh in these leaves of green.
Make me pure, make me new, make me the most precious thing you've ever seen,
And I will love Thee.

And I will sacrifice.

And I will climb down to tell the others what it can be like to dwell above

As the snakes are at our feet, slithering about, hissing their message of "love."

A divine branch shall then extend itself, light reaching out and all around.

Meanwhile, the "church" is here—the para-structure—uniting the nations, and their troops are on the ground,

Killing and preaching.

The renewal of our concept of soul, burning all from which it came.

Burning these numbers, these illusions, these equations, all thus ending in vain.

Because, you see, it is that we all truly must stem from the One,

While the devil—the empty denominator, the duplicitous demon—spawns a zero sum,

Absent fangs that somehow strike and sink into nothingness.

And that's no way to live, yet surely a way to die.

Science continuously changing; One, the constant in the sky.

Yes, they continue to challenge with evidence contrary, a damning proclamation of thyself.

So in turn, it damages us, the unit, the whole, we as one; singularity a virtue of wealth.

The likeness, the image of humanity distorted and out of view.

For here we are, a pile of ash, payment for all we thought we knew,

And we should know better.

Our families before understood, so that's why it's more terrifying to see it torn apart.

A family accepting the sanctity of bread, seated at the table, now a lost form of art.

And here is life, the imitation of color, blurring before our very eyes.

As we give no thanks and say no grace, fire consumes our family ties.

And so yes, ignite this rabble down to this very pile of ash

Right here upon this earth, where the "church" once stood,

Some made of steel, many made of stone, but most made of wood.

And then, from there on out, we, the leftover body, shall continue looking to Thine head,

Dwelling in Your forest, drinking from Your river, and feasting on Thine bread,

Giving thanks in fellowship—koinonia.

Awaiting the cosmic reconciliation.

Yours truly,

The Church

SKULL

Does it move you?
And if so, in what direction?
These fated paces
We can never know for sure.
But does it move you?
And if so, let it nudge you a little more
Into the river, unto the ocean, unto this wave.
Let the miracle wash over you.
This water, endowed it be to save.
And here, yes, one will assuredly drown, but there be no need to mourn
For we, caught up in the riptide, fear not death nor the impending storm.
And our necks will not weary as the swords of our slayers grow dull.
Blessed be thy spirit, risen.
Departed, on the shore remains
Thy skull.

CREATION

Born of loneliness,
A longing for another,
The acceptance of the other.
Transgression
Toward the mean.
Murder by numbers.
The blade never be at fault.
It just keeps one from using their hands,
Opposable
Thumbs to the eyes of the Everyman
And all the "apes" alike.
From a pedestal, one creates
Idols,
Demons,
Celebrities,
gods,
Art.
And so,
Blood be the ink,
Flesh be the paper.
Thine will be thine pen.
Clay thrown into the fire.
All is justified.
All is conquered.
As all is forgiven
In the end.

POETRY FOR THE END
OF THE WORLD

It began with the dawn, the rise, an ill-fated dream.
"Apes" from out the ooze? A big bang? And thus, a primal scream,
A call, a cry into the dark, our lost sacred tribe howling at the moon.
As we tried to understand this thing called life, in our banishment, we built a fire,
light for our padded rooms.
Learning our shapes; that's a circle, that yellow thing in the sky.
"Look at that thing with wings." Man, how we wish we could fly.
But first what do we call these things? How can I communicate with you?
Out our mouths shot syllables, sounds forming words: "birds" fly because we say
they do.
We humans, well, what do we do?
Ha! Well, we go to war.
Complex creatures creating chaos, feeling inferior.
Unto each other; unto ourselves, unto this scene.
The landscape, sculpted by the Creator, the Director, Producer, and Star of our ill-
fated dream.
In our minds, we cease to believe.
In our minds, we cease to achieve.
Our new dawn, our second chance, our last handheld walk in the park.
A nightingale sang to me of our demise; it was I alone, strolling after dark.
In my shortness of breath, my aching heart, my rushing blood, my blinking eyes,
I saw death on the horizon, I saw destruction, I saw shapes melting there as they lie.
Face-down, crying into their palms, feeling they truly gave it their best.
This human race coming to an end; saving ourselves seemingly our final test.
Our greatest war, our finest hour, our one collaborative good deed.
Our mission to save our starving souls for upon Your earth we must plant the seed.
The idea that our story—our love affair, our species, our home—could all come to
an end.
The wheel, setting our world in motion, turning us around and around again and
again.
Our spark, our revolution.
Our pride in the name of evolution—and so we regress.
In the name of man, we write our memoirs, we the spectators of life, negligible to
our biggest fan.

Slipping away, falling through time and space, we, eight billion grains of sand.
Lost, looking for love, fulfillment and purpose in our time of dying.
Time, the concept we created, continues to keep on flying
Into the black, into the abyss, into the distance, into the blue.
In my cave, I sit, a product of existential nostalgia,
Writing poetry for the end of the world and thinking of all of you.
Of us,
My people,
My brethren,
My blood,
My kin.
Glory be
As it was in the beginning
Is now
And ever shall be
World without end.
Amen!

CPSIA information can be obtained
at www.ICGtesting.com
Printed in the USA
LVHW032036170220
647203LV00004B/482